A Black Widow Like No Other

Belinda Patterson

Published by Trellis Publishing, 2021.

While every precaution has been taken in the preparation of this book, the publisher assumes no responsibility for errors or omissions, or for damages resulting from the use of the information contained herein.

A BLACK WIDOW LIKE NO OTHER

First edition. July 16, 2021.

Copyright © 2021 Belinda Patterson.

ISBN: 979-8224021130

Written by Belinda Patterson.

A BLACK WIDOW LIKE NO OTHER

THE TRUE STORY OF CHRISTINA BUTTON

BELINDA PATTERSON

Fifty-five years old.

George Button repeated his age over and over.

He felt guilt and shame for how little he had accomplished in life. He heard it once said that money was a reflection of your accomplishments in life. If that were true, he was in big trouble.

Or was he?

Christina kept spending more than they could afford. He tried to warn her, even going so far as to show her the overdue notices on the credit card bills. But her rebuttals would always be the same.

"So we don't deserve it? So I don't deserve it? So you're not man enough to pay the bills?"

His appeals to reason would always end with her attacking his masculinity.

Walking with his dog down the quiet street, he wished life could be this simple and routine. It cost nothing to enjoy a walk with your hound. They had enough to eat. A roof over their head (for now).

Why couldn't she see things the way he did?

The cold night clung to the clear air, just as mean and oppressive as Christina's words echoing in his head. There was no mist in the park though as there usually was. The night sky seemed almost fragile in its clarity.

He watched his dog Laddie sniffing through the grass, the blades catching the moonlight which made them look like sharpened teeth. In the trees, leaves dropped from their branches like men who have been lynched.

The nightly walks usually calmed his nerves. But on this night, it only gave him a sense of foreboding.

The running feet behind him came so fast that he didn't have time to even turn around.

All he felt was the pain. A deep red haze clouding his vision.

The blunt object came on him time and again until he fell hard on the asphalt, his blood seeping into the rain-soaked asphalt.

He didn't remember when the paramedics came. Or how long they worked on him in the emergency room.

They worked frantically to stem his bleeding but the trauma was too much.

George Button was dead.

"It was a hit and run," the paramedics pronounced.

But they were wrong. Dead wrong.

"A little backstory..."

George worked as an electrician for the city council when he met Christina. He had never married and had spent the last several years caring for his aging parents. When they died, he came into an inheritance.

When Christina found out how much money he inherited, she immediately began flirting with the overweight but friendly George whom everyone called "The Gentle Giant."

Christina was twenty-two years the junior of George when they got married. He was smitten with the blonde woman and the amount of attention she gave him.

They would have a little girl together and George loved her dearly, doting on both of the women in his life.

But Christina would soon take advantage of this devotion.

She would drag George out to all of the boutique shops around town, buying whatever caught her eye.

"I don't want anything cheap," Christina said as she browsed through the children's dresses.

"That's ridiculous," George said, looking at the price tag on one of the items. "Can you imagine paying this much for a dress. She's seven years old not some fashion diva."

"What's wrong with it?" Christina demanded. "Do you want your daughter to look like she just escaped from the poor house? We're buying it."

"Gotta to be something-"

"Cheaper?"

"More reasonable."

"Reasonable is being like everyone else," Christina said. "You always say I'm special. You always tell your daughter she's special. But when it comes to doing something special you always come up with an excuse. I just wish that for once you would see things the way I do."

"But we can't afford it-"

"Fine!" Christina said, throwing the dress down.

George blushed as people in the store turned their heads. He hated to make her upset. Her tone of voice. But it was the way she looked at him that made his heart hurt. A facial expression of irrational and inconsolable anger. She was mad at everything about him. A look that said she hated him as much as he loved her.

"We can't afford anything. Not with George," she scoffed.

The mounds of George's wide shoulders drooped as if the air had been punched out of him.

"Okay."

"Okay, what?"

"Buy what you need."

Minutes later, George trailed behind his young wife as she made her way to the cash register armed with the latest fashions for herself and her daughter.

George always gave in. He felt inferior to Christina in so many ways. He thought she could have any man she wanted but she picked him. But if he stopped paying for stuff she would leave him. Maybe she would even take their daughter with her. He knew how the courts operated.

The mortgage was already draining them dry even with both of them working now. The bill collectors were starting to call the house. Christina had over fourteen credit cards and had maxed out every single one.

They needed money.

They had dug themselves into a hole of debt. The problem was Christina wanted to keep on digging.

"Stealing from the job..."

"Hon," Christina used her sweet voice when she needed something.

"What is it, babe?" George said as he answered his cell phone. He was always happy and surprised when she called him.

"What's wrong?"

"Can you come down to my job?"

"What's wrong?"

"I'll explain when you get here-"

She hung up the phone, not wanting to explain further.

Christina had gotten caught. The manager at the company she worked for couldn't help but notice that a considerable amount of money was missing from the company's account.

Although George was lenient about Christina's spending habits. Her boss wouldn't be.

He demanded to know what Christina did with the money. After about ten minutes of interrogation, she relented. She admitted that she stole the money.

The boss was beside himself. He threatened to call the police.

Christina pleaded with him to not get the authorities involved. That if she could just call her husband he would know how to fix this.

Her manager did have a soft heart. He knew that Christina had a young daughter and that times were tight. But if her husband wouldn't agree to pay the money back...

When George was apprised of the situation, he didn't hesitate. The idea of having his beautiful wife locked up in a jail cell was out of the question. He agreed to pay the amount she had stolen.

There was no other way, he rationalized to himself as they drove back home in silence.

Christina was now out of a job and had put the family further down the hole financially.

George thought she would somehow repay him for his gratitude. To be thankful for bailing her out of a situation where she could have easily have went to prison.

But nothing.

When they arrived home, Christina acted as if nothing was wrong. In fact, she ignored him as they went up the steps and immediately went to her room.

George didn't know what to do. He could only work so many hours. He began looking around the house for things he could pawn until he realized that every single knick-knack was purchased by Christina who would go ballistic if he sold any of 'her' stuff

He slouched on the sofa and turned on the television. Flipping the stations, he desperately wanted to find something that would help him escape.

Christina, on the other hand, went straight into the shower. She made the water as hot as she could endure as she spent a good five minutes just enjoying the heat.

Out of the shower, she swiped her hand over the bathroom mirror, making a clear streak across the fogged surface. The reflection staring back at her was the same as yesterday.

That amazed Christina. That no matter what she did, she would look the same.

"Not a worry wrinkle at all," Christina said, admiring herself in the mirror.

"Visitors..."

Her friend Stephanie stopped by and Christina mentioned casually that they had remortgaged the home. Taking out what remaining equity they had, George used the money to pay off the debt incurred by Christina's theft at her job.

Of course, Christina wouldn't mention that to Stephanie as they sipped wine in front of the fireplace.

George stepped into the living room to kiss his wife goodbye. She turned her cheek to him, not wanting a smooch on the lips.

"I'll be on my way," George said, hurt at his wife's coldness.

"Overtime?" Stephanie asked.

"The second job," Christina held up the wine bottle. "Have to keep up with my expensive tastes."

George could barely manage a smile.

He was now reduced to delivering pizzas. At the age of fifty-five, he found the task humiliating. But they were in debt.

It was the only way.

Christina watched as George closed the door and left.

"You know, sometimes I think I only married him because I felt sorry for him."

"Really?"

"Yeah, really."

Stephanie looked around the home. She marveled at the expensive items; the furniture, the artwork, the clothing on Christina.

George made blue collar money. He was an electrician. Good job with a pension but nothing that would suggest some of the amenities she saw around the house.

"Don't get me wrong," Christina added. "I will miss him. He has over a half-million dollar life insurance policy."

The gold digger then paused for dramatic effect.

"I'll miss him for about two minutes," Christina laughed hard, drinking from her wine glass.

Stephanie could only manage a smile. "You're horrible."

"I'm sorry," she continued. "I think the wine is getting to me."

Stephanie changed the subject, choosing to talk about the latest television episode of a show Christina didn't follow.

Her mind wandered. That life insurance policy would be her ticket to a better life. Freedom from George's prying eye and a huge boost to her purse.

If only she could get rid of him.
She couldn't kill him herself. No way she'd get away with it.
No. There had to be a patsy.
In 2003, she found him.
Simon Tannahill. Her own nephew.
"A visiting relative..."
Down on his luck, Simon agreed to come live with George and his aunt Christina with the agreement that he would pay rent for a room. He had a falling out with his own parents and Christina immediately offered him a room. Not wanting any conflict with his wife, George gave the green light to the arrangement as he desperately needed the money to pay down the mortgage. Simon wouldn't be able to pay a whole lot but any little bit helped.

Christina saw something else in Simon. She saw the young man for what he was. A man who had no self-confidence and no experience with women.

A willing patsy.

The young man kept to himself for the first few days. He came and went without any fanfare. George small-talked with the young man at dinner, talking about soccer and his own favorite players.

"How do you like the steak?" Christina asked.

"Oh, it's delicious," Simon smiled.

"See?" George said. "She doesn't even cook me steak anymore."

"This is a special occasion," Christina stared into Simon's eyes until he blushed.

George then left to deliver his pizzas then Christina put her plan into motion.

She went into the bathroom and swept her blonde hair behind her ears. She applied some eyeliner and touched her lips over with a peachy-pink gloss. She took off her dowdy dress and put on a tight blouse with a few buttons undone.

Spotting Simon sitting on the living room couch, she sat down next to the young man. Close enough to where their thighs touched.

"Hey," she said.

"Hey," Simon said shyly.

"How are you liking it here so far?"

"It's great. Great. Thanks so much."

He returned his attention to the soccer match on television.

"I can't believe what a handsome man you've become," Christina said, squeezing his bicep. "And strong too."

Simon pulled his arm away, an embarrassed laugh coming from his lips.

"No girlfriend yet?"

"No."

"You can bring her here if you get one," Christina laughed then corrected herself. "When you get one."

"Thanks."

"You are a really, really handsome boy," Christina reached over and ran her fingers through the young man's hair. "I think the last time I saw you, you were around eight or nine years old."

"Sounds about right," Simon said.

"Women are going to like you," she cooed. "They are going to like you so much. Do you like me, Simon?"

"Yeah."

"I mean do you like me? I'm not bad for a woman my age, right?"

Christina undid another button of her blouse.

"No," Simon couldn't help but stare at the bare flesh revealed by the simple gesture. "I really should go to bed. I have an early day tomorrow."

Christina smiled as she watched the young man nervously walk out of the room but give her ample breasts another glance. She laughed to herself.

Her poor nephew was so inexperienced that he would probably fall in love with her if she gave him a sixty-second hand job.

"A confused young man..."

Simon found it hard concentrating at work the following day. He didn't know what to make of Christina's overture. Was she drinking? He caught her staring at him, a stare that lasted just a little too long. She was his aunt, for Chrissakes.

Then his cell phone beeped. A text message.

"Simon?"

The text was from Christina.

"Hi," he texted back.

"I saw the way you looked at me last night," came her response. A pair of heart emojis followed.

Simon's heart started to race. WTF?

"You can't help but stare at my tits, can you?"

"Christina, is this really you?"

"Don't act like you don't remember? I wore a button down baby blue blouse. I left the two three buttons undone. That was for you, Simon."

"Really?"

"Did you like what you saw?"

"Yes."

"If you do something for me, I'll show them to you. I'll show them to you and more."

"What do you mean, 'more'?"

"I mean if you want to fuck me like a jackhammer, so be it."

Simon ate dinner with the family that night. George didn't give him any strange looks but Christina played footsie with him under the table. The light from above the kitchen gave her face a luminescent glow. It flattened her features, making her expression as pale and clear as a full moon.

She wanted him.

But he went straight to his bedroom after dinner. He noodled through his cell phone again, wondering if he had imagined those text messages from Christina. This was so wrong. This was his aunt! His own aunt making a move on him.

Hearing the door slam shut, he looked out the window and watched as George got into his car.

Time to deliver pizzas.

Then he heard a knock on his door.

"Come in," he said, hesitating.

The door opened slowly.

"Simon," Christina whispered.

"Yes."

"I need you to do me a favor."

"What kind of favor-"

"Does it matter?" Christina said, leaning her elbow against the doorpost with her hand placed behind her head. A practiced pose of seduction.

What madness was this?

"I want to show you something."

"A simple plan..."

Simon sat on the driver side of the car with Christina in the passenger seat, telling which turns to take as they snaked around the country lane.

"This is a lonely road, Simon. Anyone can get away with anything here."

"What is that you had in mind?"

"I want you to kill George."

"What?"

"I want you to kill George for me."

"Why?"

"He has a life insurance policy," Christina said. "There's enough money for both of us. Then I'll be yours."

"Mine?"

"You haven't been with a woman yet have you?" she cooed, running her hand over his crotch.

Simon didn't respond. Christina's words hissed through his head like a snake, tickling the sickness of his mind and soul.

"Here," she said, taking his hand and placing it on her breast. "You like how it feels?"

"Yes," he said. His arousal added an extra layer of weirdness to what already felt like a crazy dream.

"You can make it look like an accident," Christina said. "It's so easy. Then I'll be free. Free to be with you. And we'll have so much money. So much fun."

"I don't know if I can."

"Of course you can," Christina squeezed his bicep again. "See I know your mom. She smothered you because she doesn't think much of you. Me? I know what you're capable of. You're capable of doing anything. That's what is so sexy about you."

They drove back home. Christina greeted her husband as if nothing was wrong.

But Simon couldn't sleep that night.

Christina had this hold over him, a hold that he couldn't break.

He stared up at the ceiling, watching the shadows play on the wall.

Everyone was quiet at the dinner table except the Button's young daughter, Laura. She had a day full of papier-mache and Play-doh at school, describing her creations to her father.

Then George excused himself from the dinner table and whistled for Laddie, their dog.

He followed a routine every night just as Christina instructed Simon. George would walk the dog down the lonely country road where they had reconned the night before.

Waiting until the old man left the house, Simon and Christina dashed outside and drove to the middle of the road.

They both laid in wait for the man who had to die.

I could handle this, Simon whispered to himself.

George was a large man. But he was old. Besides Christina came along.

And Christina always had all the answers.

She said nothing as she exited the vehicle. He watched as she moved behind a tree and waited.

She would be there for him.

But doubt took over as soon as he stepped outside the vehicle. The night air was shockingly cold. He rubbed his arms for warmth as his heartbeat began racing.

Looking back at Christina, he could only make out her lighting a cigarette while standing next to the tree.

He saw George up ahead. He wondered if Laddie would attack him once he began hitting his uncle.

The anxiety increased as did his walking pace. It was as if some dark force was propelling him forward.

Christina.

The wrongness of the situation became obvious to him. He felt it in his gut, as if his conscience suddenly became an internal organ, pink and shiny, flaring with a sound alarm.

We shouldn't be doing this. This is wrong.

He wished he were back home at the home of his parents. He wanted to feel taken care of again. Instead, he felt powerless and small.

He didn't have the guts to do this.

But if he didn't do it, what would Christina say?

"Wimp. Coward. Wimp. Coward. You're just like George."

Simon didn't want to grow up and be like George. He wanted to be the kind of man that woman like Christina found attractive...

Approaching from behind, Simon sprinted across the quiet road and smashed George with the club.

The weapon whipped into George so hard it jerked his head to the left.

The old man went down, the sound of his head hitting the cement sickened his nephew.

Simon's vision clouded with a red pulse of violence that blocked out all sense of right or wrong. Time contracted and he was lost in a dark tunnel that he fell through, as he clubbed down at his benefactor with all his might. The blood splattered across the asphalt.

Christina watched from afar. Satisfied, she ditched her cigarette and hopped in the vehicle driving over to Simon.

Her nephew, seemingly in a daze, snapped out of his funk when he saw the headlights cruising up.

He practically dove into the passenger side of the car, wanting to cling to Christina. He laid the club on the dash as they calmly drove back to their residence.

Christina watched in the rearview mirror as a passerby stopped in front of George's motionless body. She wanted the car to run over her husband, just to be certain.

Simon looked back himself. His guilt ticked up another notch.

George was nothing but good to him.

Now he was alone on the street, dying

He curled his fingers around the club again, closing his eyes. Cursing himself for what he's done.

Inhaling a deep, jittery breath. "What now?"

"We wait," Christina whispered.

He looked over at her.

She looked beautiful and curvy, the street lights tracing the line of her jaw. An air of dark mystery radiated off her.

Then her hair fell from behind her ears and covered her face, like a protective veil.

A fresh wave of fear crashed over Simon.

"An Oscar award-winning performance..."

The police notified Christina within a few hours. She was told it was a hit and run. After an emergency surgery, George was unable to make it through the night.

Christina bawled in grief upon hearing the news. She dropped to the floor and the policemen tried to lift her up.

"Not George!" she cried. "Not my Georgie!"

At the funeral, she continued her to play-act the role of a grieving widow. Relatives would come up and express their condolences, hugging the inconsolable Christina.

On his grave, she left him a bouquet of flowers with a note.

"I love you. I love you."

But police knew better.

Their forensic team had noticed that George had wounds to the back of his head that were consistent with that blunt force trauma rather than being hit by a vehicle.

Keeping their cards close to their chest, the police began to trail Christina. They would question Simon and discover the 'sexting' exchange between the two of them.

He immediately became a person of interest.

The police obtained a search warrant and found traces of George's blood in his vehicle.

Both Christina and Simon would be arrested, tried and convicted. In 2003, Simon would be sentenced to life in prison. Christina would be sentenced to a minimum of fourteen years. Upon hearing the verdict, she immediately "fainted" in the courtroom.

"Incorrigible..."

While in prison, Christina would send letters protesting her innocence to Susan, one of her sisters.

"My impression of the law has changed greatly," Christina wrote. "I now feel that there is so much corruption, dishonesty, and betrayal. I think they (the police) have forgotten exactly what their job description says. I will never trust the police again as long as I live."

But Susan always knew that Christina was a liar and refused to placate her sister's insistence that she was the victim of a conspiracy.

"It actually feels like a personal vendetta against me now," Christina wrote. "I feel like they know they have made a mistake, so they are desperate to turn people against me and discredit me."

In another letter, Christina vented her anger toward her older sister.

"All I would ask of you Susan is to think before you speak," Christina wrote. "I know you mean well and are just trying to help me. But, if you really want to help me, you'll just have to keep yourself to yourself, which I know is very hard....Don't go shouting your mouth off to anyone; friends, medical staff and police about this."

Susan would later reveal that Christina warned against her coming to George's funeral. She informed Susan that the service would only be for her and their daughter Laura to attend.

But Susan knew it was a lie. Over three hundred people attended the service for the man who everyone knew as the "Gentle Giant."

When Christina came up for parole, her letters to Susan have increased as she wanted her older sister to keep out of her legal situation.

"She goes on about how she's innocent," Susan said. "But Christina is very, very manipulative and cunning. My family doesn't speak to me anymore, they tell people I'm dead, but I want to make sure Christina serves her time for what she did to George."

Christina caused further controversy while in jail when she decided to have a breast reduction surgery at the expense of the taxpayer.

She went on a fasting diet and lost over forty pounds of weight. The medical staff at the jail approved her operation to tighten her skin. The surgery cost taxpayers well over ten thousand dollars.

"She has been bragging about this operation for some time now," an anonymous source in the prison said. "She was very fat for ages but has gone on a diet and lost loads of weight. As a result, she has loose skin and wants this surgery to change that. We can't believe the taxpayer is being asked to fork out for a killer's vanity. She is not very popular in the prison. She pretends to be people's friends but nobody trusts her."

"When I get out," Christina said. "I'm going to be looking good."

LOUISE PEETE

BELINDA PATTERSON

DIANE PLANT

"She's an entrepreneur. A homicidal entrepreneur."

Louise Peete was a convicted American murderer famous for becoming the second woman in history to be executed in the State of California.

She was sentenced to life in prison for the murder of a wealthy mining engineer named Jacob C. Denton in 1920. Nineteen years later, however, she would be released from prison only to kill again. In a bizarre series of crimes, she would kill one of her benefactors, a social worker named Margaret Logan and be executed for committing that murder in April of 1947.

EARLY YEARS

Peete was born on September 20th, 1880 in Bienville, Louisiana. Her father was a successful newspaper publisher. Peete later revealed that she "came from cultured, educated people. My parents were not delinquents, and did not rear delinquent children."

Louise attended a private school in New Orleans but was kicked out at the age of fifteen.

"She was the school slut," forensic psychologist Harvey Duggan said. "There is no other way to put it. At the age of fifteen she had slept with every body in the school and stole everything that wasn't nailed down, particularly jewelry. Finally, she would be expelled. But with her family's money, she would be able to survive and get numerous second chances at the straight and narrow which she never took. Eventually, I believe her family cut ties with her and that is when all hell broke loose."

Louise would travel to Boston to study singing with dreams of an operatic career. In 1903, however, she married her first husband in Henry Bosley.

"Louise was the quintessential Southern Belle, at least on the surface," Duggan explained. "She could seduce a man with her looks and charm. You would never, ever guess that she would be capable of the things she did. I would surmise that she had more than just a way with men. She had a way of getting under their skin, getting into their personal psychology and manipulating them into becoming obsessed with her. These men wanted to help her. They wanted to gain her approval. So when they experienced her rejection, they felt like failures themselves. So much so that they would take their own lives. She had that kind of power."

There are various conflicting reports on how the relationship with Bosley ended. There are some reports that he divorced her and there are others where he killed himself after finding Louise in bed with another man, a New Orleans oil magnate.

After her marriage ended, it appeared that Louise had been cut off from her family and was strapped for cash. She moved to Shreveport, Louisiana, where she worked as an upscale prostitute, servicing wealthy men. She would steal from the men and go through their wife's drawers, pilfering jewelry.

"She worked as a prostitute to save enough money for her move to Boston," Duggan said. "It remains unclear to me as to why or how she became estranged from her family. The Preslars (Louise's family) were relatively wealthy. I can only speculate that she embarrassed the family name with her escapades. So they most likely cut her off with Southern culture being what it was back then."

In 1911, Peete moved to Boston and change her name to either Louise M. Gould or Anna Lee Gould.

FOOLING THE SOCIALITES

"Louise was a master manipulator of people," FBI profiler Candice Delong said. "This started when she was a young girl."

Once in Boston, Louise began telling people that she was a 19-year-old Dallas socialite by the name of RH Rosler.

"She posed as a rich 19-year-old heiress," said Duggan. "She told people that she was placed in a convent in Los Angeles and escaped. She told people that she owned property in Norway and Germany. Because of her charm and beauty people accepted her stories. Keep in mind that these were prominent families in Boston. So there was one family that had taken her in and treated her as if she were their own daughter. Louise then proceeded to run up huge bills at some of the most expensive stores in Boston. When her fraud was discovered, Louise was allowed to leave peacefully as long as she kept her mouth shut because no one in Boston's high society wanted people to know that they had been duped. The family refused to prosecute and Louise was allowed to get away with her crime as long as she left town."

MORE THAN A HEART BREAKER

"She was this sweet, innocent person," writer Sue Pascoe said. "That everyone loved. That everyone wanted to take care of."

It is in Waco, Texas in 1913 where Louise indulged in a whirlwind romance with Joe Appel, a Yankee who made his money in Texas oil.

"She hooked up with a wealthy oil man," Pascoe said. "Who had diamonds on his belt buckles, diamonds on his buttons, diamonds everywhere. His name was Joe Appel."

"She knew how to speak to people with money," history professor Gordon Morris Bakken said. "Because she came from a family where she was surrounded by money."

A week after meeting Peete, "Diamond" Joe Appel would be found shot to death with all of his jewelry now missing.

"She shot him," Delong said. "And his diamonds disappeared. Peete was arrested, tried but released after she convinced the jury that Appel was trying to rape her and she killed him in self-defense.

"An all male jury listening to her saying that it was a 'Yankee who tried to force himself on me,'" Bakken said. "That was good enough for no indictment."

The jury applauded Louise after she explained that she shot Appel because she was "defending her honor" after he tried to rape her.

MOVING ON

"She moved to Dallas where she's running a little bit short of funds," Pascoe said. "So she hooks up with a hotel clerk, Harry Faurote."

Faurote was a hotel manager who worked at the St. George hotel. He was immediately smitten by the Southern charm of the smooth talking Louise.

"She marries him and then the pattern is repeated," Bakken said. "He catches her with other men."

Faurote did not fit the profile of Peete's usual target of men as she preferred wealthy, successful types. Faurote's usefulness to Louise, however, would soon became apparent as Peete stole over $20,000 worth of jewels from the hotel safe. Police would later question Faurote and acquit him of any wrongdoing. They knew that Peete performed the theft but could not prove it. Shamed over being accused of the theft and then catching Louise in bed with another man, Faurote committed suicide.

There are differing reports of his demise, but he either shot or hung himself in the hotel basement.

A PATTERN EMERGES

Two suicides and one man shot. Use and abuse other people. The pattern was now repeating.

"She traveled from state to state," Delong said, describing Louise's promiscuity. "Sometimes they would become lovers. Sometimes she would marry them."

Peete would then move to Denver and marry a salesman named Richard Peete.

The wedding with Richard would become the social event of the season in 1914. The two looked like a match made in heaven at the time. The United States had entered World War I and Richard was prospering as a door to door salesman. But when peace was restored, Richard's income began to slump. Bankruptcy loomed and the couple fought constantly. After six years of marriage, Louise decided to separate herself from the situation.

One morning, Richard saw Louise packing a suitcase.

"Going on a trip, my dear?" Richard asked.

"I think I need a change of air, Richard, perhaps it would be better if I took a trip to Los Angeles. It will be better for the both of us."

Adding a further complication to Louise's flight was that she had a child with Richard, a daughter named Francis Ann (nicknamed Betty) in 1916.

"She was never happy with what she had," Delong said. "She always wanted more."

CITY OF ANGELS NO MORE

While in Los Angeles, Louise would meet Jacob C. Denton.

Denton had recently lost his wife and lived alone with his teenage daughter. He had made his millions as a mining engineer and had recently retired. Denton had met Peete after she inquired about his fourteen room English two-door mansion which Denton wanted to rent out for $350 a month.

"Denton had lost his wife in the recent influenza epidemic," Duggan said. "Louise saw him as a man who would be susceptible to her Southern charm. He was old, lonely and would probably be easy pickings after a few nights of passionate sex. Louise probably did things to him in the bedroom that he had never experienced before, really rocking his world. But when she pushed him for marriage after only a week, he balked. He was a successful business with a lot to lose and was no push over. Louise, however, took the rejection in stride. She had a side plan, get the man so addicted to sex that at the very least, he would let her move in with him. Then she could put her real plan into effect"

Louise talked Denton down to $75 a month and moved in on May 26. While the relationship of Louise and Denton is muddled, as some reports have her listed as his housekeeper. This clearly was not the case, as they certainly had a beneficial relationship.

Louise graciously helped the current tenant to move out. She then invited a Denver friend, Mrs. Gregory, to spend the summer with her, asking her to arrive on June 2nd. "By that time," she told Mrs. Gregory. "Mr. Denton will be gone."

True to her word, a week after Louise moved into Denton's home, he disappeared.

A MUSHROOM GARDEN?

Shortly after Denton was declared missing, Louise made one of the gardeners transport a load of dirt to the basement of Denton's home. "I want to grow some mushrooms," she explained.

She then lured the unsuspecting Denton into the basement, showing him that she planned to grow mushrooms there.

With his back turned to her, Louise shot him in the head.

Three days later, she forged Denton's signature in order to withdraw $300 from his bank account. She also gained access to his safe deposit box.

One of the bank officials took note that the signatures did not match and confronted Louise. She explained that Denton's right arm had been amputated after he had been shot by a "mysterious Spanish woman" that he had been fighting with.

When the bank official informed her that Denton signed with his left hand, Louise doubled-down on her story by saying that Denton had gone into hiding and was "ashamed" by his amputated arm.

"He doesn't want to be seen in public just yet," Louise explained. "That's why I'm here conducting business for him."

"Louise had quite the imagination," Duggan said. "Or I should say she could be quite charming. Who would believe the stories she told? Apparently, just about everyone. She told the story that a Spanish woman had shot Denton in the arm. Then another version of the same story where the woman chopped off Denton's arm with a sword. And in another version, she would say that the woman chopped Denton's leg off. When pressed for his whereabouts, she would tell his friends that

Denton would come out of hiding once he learned how to use his new prosthetic limbs."

"With Denton out of the way, it was time to party. She called herself 'Mrs. Denton' and threw parties in the home, all financed from his money. She was the classic sociopath, using people then throwing them away. With the parties, for some reason, it seemed that she wanted to be seen as better than what she really was, throwing all that money around."

THE SEARCH FOR JACOB DENTON

In the following weeks, all of Denton's friends, business partners and neighbors began pestering Louise about his whereabouts. Louise would explain Denton's absence by saying that he was on a business trip and had to go to various locations but would be back shortly. During this time, she enjoyed access to Denton's money and drove around town in his Cadillac. She's sold his jewelry and other items, rented out rooms in his mansion and pocketed the rent money. Additionally, Denton owned rental properties in Phoenix and Louise contacted his tenants there. She then informed them to make out the rent checks to her.

"She gave them the story about his arm," Duggan said. "The tenants bought it hook, line and sinker, sending her the checks."

Louise then charged two expensive dresses at Bullock's department store to Denton's account as she told them she was his wife.

Denton had a fifteen-year-old daughter named Francis who in May 1920 received a letter from Denton stating that he would be visiting her in Phoenix on June 1st. Denton never showed up and after two weeks his daughter went to his law firm and told them of his absence. A judge then called the Denton home in Los Angeles out of concern. Louise told the judge that Denton had left the house on business and that she expected to hear from him soon. By September, however, Denton had still not turned up anywhere.

"What happened was Louise had worked her charm," Duggan said. "The authorities waited over four months before they came into investigate. Louise had no doubt relieved them of any suspicion with her polite Southern manner. No one would think that she would be capable of any wrong doing, that sweet Southern girl who spoke with such caring and kindness."

The Denton family attorney, a man named Rush Blodgett, demanded that Louise send him Denton's financial and business documents as soon as possible. Feeling the heat, Louise returned to Denver to rejoin her husband Richard and daughter.

Blodgett hired a private detective named A.J. Cody who searched the home. They found Denton's decomposing body in the basement.

The man's body had been placed in a wooden cubicle under the stairs. An autopsy revealed that he had been shot in the head and strangled. His body was bound up in numerous cords and wrapped up in a quilt.

The police tracked Louise down in Denver and interrogated her about Denton's murder. She maintained her innocence but offered different scenarios to explain his death. Louise claimed that the unidentified "mysterious Spanish woman" that shot Denton in the arm had also been his killer. This claim was later dismissed as Denton's body was found with his right arm uninjured. Despite Louise's claim that a gunshot wound required that his arm be amputated, Denton's arm was found to be still attached to his body.

Louise doubled-down on her story again. She stated that the body that the police found was not Denton but a body double that Denton had killed himself. Not buying her outlandish story, the LAPD brought Louise back to Los Angeles where she found herself indicted for first degree murder.

"She went back to live with her husband Richard and daughter in Denver," Duggan said. "The Los Angeles Police Department did not buy any of Louise's Southern belle charm as they found jewelry and furs that belonged to Denton in her possession. Again, she was a charming criminal but not a very smart one as she had a laughable inability to cover her own tracks."

Under questioning, Louise could not properly explain why she had purchased the two dresses under the name of "Mrs. JC Denton" as well as the parties and broken furniture in the Denton home. She had been consulted by her attorney not to "over talk" but Louise could not resist.

Given a platform she never had before, she told reporters that she was being crucified: "I am being crucified upon a cross. But I can say, as did Christ, 'Father, forgive them, for they know not what they do.'"

"But the LAPD knew exactly what they were doing," Duggan said. "They found the gun in the closet where Louise's dresses were. They knew they had their killer."

THE TRIAL

On January 21st, 1921 her trial began, a media circus from the get-go. Newspapers nationwide covered the trial on front pages, dubbing her as the "Tiger Woman." Thousands of onlookers stood outside the court daily, hoping to catch a glimpse of the murderous woman that they read about.

Louise, however, had dodged a murder charge before and was confident she could do it again.

"You have this sweet, Southern belle projecting innocence," Pascoe said. "Like 'oh my goodness,' you can imagine what happened."

Her trial lasted until February 17th, 1921 when she was convicted of first-degree murder and sentenced to life imprisonment.

"The all male jury found Louise Peete guilty," Bakken said. "And recommended a sentence to the judge of life in prison."

Her husband Richard Peete remained loyal throughout the trial and maintained her innocence. Louise told Richard that he should divorce her so that he can be free to remarry. Richard granted her the divorce but promised that he would "wait forever" for her to be released from prison. After the divorce was finalized, the imprisoned Louise no longer answered Richard's letters.

He would come to the jail and she would refuse to see him. Heartbroken over her rejection, Richard shot himself in an Arizona hotel room in 1924. Louise would say later to reporters that her ex-husband killed himself because he felt guilty over her conviction and was despondent over his own failing health.

According to accounts in prison, however, Louise was really pleased with the fact that she had that much power over a man. She bragged about it to her fellow inmates. The warden at the time described her as projecting an air of innocence and sweetness while masking a heart of ice.

IMPRISONMENT

Louise was jailed at San Quentin State prison but later transferred to the California Institution For Women in Tehachapi, California. She made herself out to be a model prisoner, finding work inside as a dental assistant. She also took care of the flower garden and wrote in the prison newspaper.

Still, she felt above it all and recounted her disapproval of her fellow inmates to a visiting reporter.

"There should be some way of segregating the better educated, more refined women from those who have been brought up in close touch with life's slime and filth," Louise said. "They should be protected against being sullied by it."

All told, Louise served eighteen years for the murder of Jacob C. Denton. She was paroled in 1939 for good behavior.

"Louise Peete had gained weight," Bakken said. "And she wasn't the same attractive Louise Peete she was in 1921. But she was equally articulate."

She was released into the custody of Jessie Marcy, a woman who had lobbied for her release. Louise then began working for Marcy as a live-in housekeeper. Marcy then died of natural causes shortly after

Louise's release. The circumstance surrounding Marcy's death remain open for questioning, however.

Louise then moved in with her probation officer, Emily Latham, acting as her nurse and housekeeper. Similar to Marcy, Latham would die unexpectedly in 1943.

"Latham would die because of injuries related to a fall," Duggan said. "Rest assured, Louise had something to do with that. The police were unaware of Louise's history so I'm sure these deaths were not looked into in any depth. Louise had changed her name to 'Anna Lee', who was her favorite movie star. So the authorities had no idea that they were dealing with Louise Peete, convicted murderer."

NO GOOD DEED IS LEFT UNPUNISHED

Louise then moved to Pacific Palisades and lived with an elderly couple, Arthur and Margaret Logan. Louise had met Margaret while she was in jail. The two struck up a friendship and Margaret invited her to come live with them.

Margaret believed that Louise was innocent and had lobbied for her release throughout her jail term. Ironically, she also cared for Louise's daughter during her imprisonment and Richard's subsequent suicide.

Louise worked for the couple as a live-in housekeeper and became a nurse to Arthur who was suffering from dementia.

"Louise bared her soul to the Logan's," Pascoe said. "She told Margaret and Arthur everything about her past so that they would not be surprised and know everything."

Louise also continued to date, and on May 2nd, 1944 she married a banker named Lee Borden Judson. Louise did not offer the same courtesy to Judson as she did Margaret Logan. She never told Judson that she was a convicted murderer that had just spent the last eighteen years in a jail cell.

After Louise began working for the Logan's she began telling neighbors that the demented Arthur had fits of rage and would routinely attack both her and Margaret.

"This was a huge red flag," Duggan said. "Louise was setting up Margaret. When something 'bad' happened to her benefactor, she could easily point the finger of blame at Arthur as she had already greased the wheels for that to happen."

On June 1st, 1944 Margaret Logan would be reported missing.

"I think that Margaret sensed that she had made a mistake by hiring Louise," Delong said. "I think there is a special place in hell for people who take advantage of the elderly and infirmed. When Louise met Mr and Mrs. Logan, she did it all."

"At some point, Louise had gotten hold of a gun," Duggan said. "She convinced Margaret to commit Arthur to Penn State Hospital. Arthur was seventy-four years old and in the early stages of dementia. Margaret did as she was told, committing him but then changing her mind. Louise then told Margaret that she had a $100,000 trust fund in Denver that she was getting ready to inherit. She did this so she could borrow $2000 from Margaret."

"After finding her jewelry missing and some checks forged in her name, Margaret finally confronted Louise. Louise then responded by shooting Margaret in the neck and beating her with the butt of the gun."

Louise would bury Margaret's body in a shallow grave under her favorite avocado tree. She then dropped off the infirmed Arthur back at the hospital, having him recommitted.

Louise now enjoyed free reign of the Logan's assets, cashing their checks and selling off their personal belongings.

Her inability to cover her tracks, however, continued to be her undoing.

"It turns out that there was one astute parole officer," Pascoe said. "He noticed that the reports about Louise were glowing and getting better and better as the months went on. And then he happened to notice that the signatures didn't quite match."

Neighbors then began asking about Margaret's whereabouts and Louise claimed that Arthur had attacked his wife in a rage, biting her nose off. She informed them that Margaret was now in seclusion for plastic surgery and would return to public life once she felt comfortable.

Her new husband became suspicious as well, asking Louise about Margaret's whereabouts and she regaled him with tales of the violent Arthur.

For the next six months, Louise and her new husband lived in the Logan's home. Louise then began spending the Logan's money and forging their names on checks. Six months later, Arthur would die in Penn State Hospital.

Telling the hospital authorities that she was his "foster sister", Louise donated Arthur Logan's body for, in her words, "science and research."

A neighbor said Louise had done a hat dance when she learned of Arthur Logan's death in the state hospital. The neighbor said that she had erroneously received a telegram about his death and delivered the news to Louise next door.

"She read it and ran into the bedroom," the neighbor recalled. "She came out with several hats and started doing a little dance while trying them on. I stood there amazed at her reaction and she quieted down."

The neighbor then said that Louise said that she was trying on the hats for Arthur's funeral.

FORGERY REVEALED

After Arthur's death, bank officials detected one of the forgeries that Louise had made. The police were called and an investigation ensued.

On December 20th, 1944, six months after Margaret disappeared, police dug up her decomposing body under the avocado tree in the backyard of the home. Louise was arrested and charged with her murder. During interrogation, Louise claimed that Margaret was beaten and shot by her husband Arthur during a "homicidal frenzy".

Louise would admit that she buried Margaret but that she had no hand in killing her. She said that she didn't report the murder because she was afraid that she would be blamed to her due to her previous conviction. An autopsy later determined that Margaret had been shot in the back of the head and sustained a skull fracture

"The prosecutors were able to tell the jurors about Louise's history," Delong said. "And they came up with one and one equals two. Louise was a killer."

Judson was also arrested and charged with murder. But both husband and wife maintained their own innocence. On January 11th, 1945, Judson was released due to insufficient evidence.

"It was inexplicable that Judson didn't know what was going on," Duggan said. "He was probably so brainwashed and in denial that he ignored the warning signs. Louise could be that convincing, especially to a man that she had tamed through her own sexual dominance. He was like putty in her hands."

The day after Judson was released from custody, he committed suicide, jumping from the ninth floor of the Spring Arcade, an office building in Los Angeles.

When informed of her husband's latest suicide, Louise began to cry.

"I'm to blame for that," Louise said. "He couldn't face disgrace. As long as I was associated with him, he was a marked man."

"Our life together was so beautiful. He told me if you leave me, I'll take sleeping powder."

EXECUTION

On April 23rd, 1945 the trial began in Los Angeles. Newspapers described the once sexy Louise as looking "matronly" as she arrived "neatly attired in a blue suit and wearing two veils."

She waved at photographers as she entered the courtroom. "I'm humiliated but not nervous," she would say later.

Prosecutors theorized that Louise wanted control of the Logan's money. They became convinced that Louise had killed Margaret after her benefactor discovered that she had forged a $200 check in her name.

During the prosecution's opening statement, Louise yelled, "it's a lie" when the prosecutor said she had beaten Logan after shooting her. The Los Angeles Times described her as a "a plump and graying defendant," and "steely eyed."

During the trial, Louise angrily shouted and interrupted a prosecution witness.

At the end of the proceedings, Louise accused deputy district attorney John Barnes of "heckling" her during cross-examination. Barnes was known as the "Hatchet Man" because of his questioning of witnesses.

"Mrs. Peete was a Dr. Jekyll and Mrs. Hyde," Barnes told jurors. "She must've sat in a prison cell all those years, figuring out what went wrong the first time in plotting a new crime."

A jury of twelve men had found Louise guilty of murder in 1920 with a recommendation of mercy. But in 1945 a jury of eleven women and one man found her guilty of murder and made no recommendation, making the death penalty merit mandatory.

After the trial, Louise thanked reporters for their kindness and told a woman reporter who was about to cry, "don't wait for me dear."

"After she was sentenced to death," Duggan said. "Louise was a cool customer. In no way did she look like a broken spirit or a panic stricken victim. She resumed her Southern girl charm and seemed flattered at the attention that all the reporters were giving her. She even opened a gold wrapped box of chocolates and invited them all to eat the sweets as if they were at a party."

As the verdict was announced, Louise took the pronouncement with casual indifference. She sat in the courtroom reading "The Importance of Living", the Chinese philosophy book by Lin Yu Tang. She looked up from the book briefly, made a "mocking facial expression" at Barnes and then continued to read from the book.

After her conviction, Louise would tell anybody who would listen that she was innocent. She made several appeals all of which were rejected.

Louise was smug until the end, believing that California Governor Earl Warren would grant her a stay of execution.

"Warren is a gentleman," Louise said. "And a gentleman would never let a lady die in the gas chamber."

Days later, Louise's assessment would be proven wrong.

Ironically, she had left the prison decades earlier only to be returned for her execution.

She was greeted at the gas chamber door by San Quentin Warden Duffy.

"Welcome, Mrs. Peete," Duffy said. "I'm sorry to see you here. Is there anything I can do for you?"

Louise became enraged.

"Mr. Duffy," she hissed. "It might interest you to know that those guards kept me handcuffed all the way here from Tehachapi. I've never been so humiliated!"

Louise entered the gas chamber on the morning of April 11th, 1947 with a smile.

She walked lady-like into the chamber, sighing and projecting an indignant posture as if all of the proceedings were beneath her. Though calm on the outside, witnesses described her hands as trembling.

Right before the gas pellets fell, Louise turned to Warden Duffy and through the gas chamber glass she mouthed the words "thank you".

According to the Los Angeles Times, Louise had died "alone and hot." They noted that some had described her as "magnificent" at her execution.

"If that she were, it was the macabre, merciless, 'magnificent' medicines that have marked career murder, feeding and duplicity. It was more defiance and coldness than 'magnificence.'"

The Times reported that Louise's last moments in the gas chambers as follows: "(She) sniffed for the almond perfume of destiny. She threw her head back and coughed. A single white light over the chamber door flooded her face with power. (Louise) fought to keep her head high, as if a proud tragedy in the final curtain call. (When she died) her face had changed no more than a mask."

"At least she was gracious, even at the end," said a witnessing reporter in amusement.

"Yeah," said another reporter. "That lady had manners that killed."

Louise is interred at Angelus-Rosedale Cemetery in Los Angeles.

"Women like Louise have existed throughout history," Delong said. "And they always will. Buyer beware."

BLACK WIDOW : The True Story of DENA THOMPSON

BRIANNA WELLS

Dena Thompson is a woman who held power over every man that had the misfortune of falling for her charms.

Dubbed a psychopath, Dena succeeded in fooling everyone around her, including investigators, with her lies and charm for over twenty years.

Dena would post to Lonely Hearts columns and lure a steady stream of lovers and husbands into her world, eventually leaving each one emotionally and financially bankrupt.

Her first husband lost everything to her and wound up as a desperate man on the run from a mafia threat that did not exist. With one husband gone and his money spent, Thompson would go on to bigamously marry Julian Webb, a successful advertising salesman. In three short years, Mr. Webb would be found dead in his bed from an unexplainable drug overdose. Thompson's third and final husband would soon be fighting for his life when she suddenly attacked him with a bat. Still, somehow, this master manipulator would convince an entire jury that she was nothing less than the victim of abuse. No matter how many fruitless chases she sent investigators on, Thompson would not be able to keep the family members and friends of her victims from stringing the pieces together one at a time.

Her crimes were finally brought into the light of day and she would be imprisoned for her killings.

EARLY LIFE

Dena Thompson was born Dena Holmes in 1960 to a lower middle class family from Hendon, London. Her parents were named Michael and Margaret Holmes. Her father had previously worked as a prison officer but had since retired, and her mother lived as a housewife. Her childhood and teenage years held no indication of unhappiness or abuse and she graduated from school with the highest marks. Her life moved by uneventfully until, at the age of 22, she began a career with the Woolwich building society and met Lee Wyatt on a blind date set up by his cousin, Bob Reed, in 1982. On October 12th the following year, the two married in a registry office and moved into a house just below the South Downs. A small village, Dena and Lee's neighbors describe the quaint area as a "very friendly, happy place to live."

Jackie Howells, a neighbor, described the two, saying: "They were ok. You know, just ordinary neighbors when they first moved here."

Pete Howells, Jackie's husband, recalled that Mr. Wyatt was a relatively private man. "Lee kept himself to himself. You know, [polite] enough to say good morning, um, the usual things, but he was never there long enough to build up a conversation with."

Five years later, in 1987, the seemingly happy couple brought a son into the world named Darren.

Lee was an avid toy enthusiast and established the Denalee Crafts company, combining both of their names. The company would distribute hard and soft toys successfully for a time.

For extra income, Dena continued her second job working for the Woolwich building society in Arundel. Taking inspiration from the success of popular cartoon characters and the money behind merchandising, Lee worked to make his fortune by developing a soft toy character for use in cartoon films.

Their shared endeavor would prove not to be the life changing decision they thought it to be, however, when the firm went belly up and Lee was forced to allow his father-in-law to set him up with a new job at the Bedford Hotel in Brighton. Little did Lee know, that this business failure would flip a previously unseen switch in Dena's heart, hurtling her down a dark path of sex, fraud, bigamy, and murder.

Realizing that her seemingly imminent riches were gone before they began, Dena got her first taste of fraud when she began helping herself to the first installments of 26,000 pounds from the Woolwich building society. At the same time, she began to cast her eyes outward for a new man that could bring her success where she felt her current husband had failed. She soon met and began a passionate affair with Julian Webb, whom she met when he visited her office to sell advertising for the West Sussex Gazette.

Julian put forward the idea of doing a makeover using make up and clothing from local businesses in order to bring in customers. At Julian's suggestion, Dena became the model for this idea, and she was very much in love with the new work.

Julian was an active man, an avid bodybuilder and fisherman until he began a relationship with Dena. Soon, his only hobby was to please his new woman.

Peter Howells describes the moment he first saw Dena with Julian , saying: "One day, looking out the back door, [I] just happened to see Dena and another man kissing on the back doorstep, which was rather strange to say the least."

Dena loved the adrenaline rush of both stealing money and cheating on her husband. It was like a drug for her and attaining this kind of "high" would go on to dominate every action she took for the rest of her adult life.

OUT WITH THE OLD, IN WITH THE NEW

Rosemary Webb, Julian's mother, knew very little about Dena when she and Julian came to her with the announcement that they wanted to marry. Understandably, Rosemary was "a bit taken aback at the speed of this, as they'd only met last May," and they had announced their intentions in August of the same year. Only a fortnight later, wedding cards could be seen decorating the front windows of Dena's home. Neighbors were more than a little confused, since Dena Wyatt was already married. No one had seen Lee in weeks and it was as if he disappeared off the face of the earth.

Julian and Dena married on December 2nd, 1991, and Julian did not know that the marriage was bigamous.

Without Julian's knowledge, Dena had sent her first husband running for the hills only months before their marriage. Dena and Lee had signed up for the mortgage on their home together in Yapton, West Sussex. Three months later, in the year of 1991, Dena would give her husband stunning news. She claimed the two needed to separate because Lee was about to come into a large fortune, as there was allegedly a multi-million dollar deal being set up with Walt Disney over his stuffed toy named "Shaun the Leprechaun."

She told him that the mafia was now out to kill him for a cut of the money.

In order to make the lie more believable to Lee, as well as their friends and family, Dena forged letterheads from well-known toy company in the U.S. and showed them to her husband, writing up a lucrative contract that only required his signature.

Lee fell so completely for the deception that he quit his job at the Bedford Hotel.

On June 30th, a debt collector appeared at the door. Dena told her husband to run for his life while she intercepted the man. Lee would run out the back door, praying he would get away unscathed.

Fearing for his family's well-being, Lee Wyatt went on the lamb, but Dena would not allow him to fully disappear without also convincing him to write a series of letters framing himself for the Woolwich building society fraud as she continued to steal more and more money through false accounts.

In an interview taken years later, Lee was quoted saying: "She lives a life of lies and fantasy, and I was the mug who went along with it."

Lee Wyatt gave himself a new name after going on the lamb, Collin Mitchel, and sought work in the Cornish seaside resort of Newquay.

The man that eventually gave him work, David Rodd, was the manager of Carousel Amusements. He stated that Lee came in "to get away from his life in West Sussex, which was nothing strange at the time because a lot of people work for the summer, or something like that." Employees described the mysterious man as easy going and easy to talk to, happy to go out with coworkers for drinks. The job even came with a flat above the establishment that Lee rented for a place to stay. When coworkers eventually learned of his true identity much later, they were more than a little shocked.

A coworker, Mark Pope, laughed about the absurdity of such a sudden revelation, stating in an interview: "Maybe that's why when we were shouting 'Collin' he wasn't replying. We thought he might have been a little bit deaf."

For three years, Lee hid from the invisible boogeymen his cheating wife had created.

Dena, on the other end, set up shop with Julian in the house that Lee had purchased.

Lee sent most of the money he earned to his wife while he lived as a vagrant, believing that any moment his wife would call him, let him know the danger had passed, and finally tell him he could return home to the loving wife and son that awaited him. Dena, however, held no intentions of allowing him to do so, using the money he sent to fund her second wedding and even going so far as to create a gang of fictional assassins called "The G-Men" that were constantly on the hunt for their prey.

Each time Lee called home, praying that at last the "hunt" had been called off, Dena would insist he stay hidden.

Her current beau, Julian, would not be her only suitor during this time as neighbors would recount other men coming in and out of the home while her husband was away at work. There were even a few close calls in which a visitor would be leaving the home almost at the same time as Julian pulled in for lunch, something he did daily.

Christopher Cordess, a legal adviser on Dena Webb's case, had this to say of her: "She has an enormous ability to project, but this is an intense form of it. It had a sort of psychotic flavor, that is a crazy flavor, so intense that it makes people by some extraordinary mechanism -which I can't explain- has an influence over people that makes them do things which their normal selves would never do or do again."

LIES, LIES AND MORE LIES

Early on in her marriage with Julian, Dena informed her husband that she was terminally ill, and that her employer was threatening to fire her because she had taken so many days away from work due to her sickness.

Julian saw this as outrageous as Dena would look the part, acting weak and lethargic. In reality, however, Dena was being fired because 26,000 pounds were missing from accounts at the Woolwich building society, and she was being investigated for it. She claimed that her first husband, Lee, had returned and had been threatening her, blaming him for the missing money. Dena alleged that her first husband was sending her threatening letters and even secretly recorded him making threatening phone calls to her.

Dena then claimed to her neighbors, the Howells, that Lee had come to her home and raped her. The police took her false accusations seriously, and Lee Wyatt finally became the wanted man he had always wrongly believed he was.

Furious of his situation, Lee returned home whilto confront Dena while Julian was upstairs sleeping. Dena refused to explain anything and managed to turn him away. Little did she know that her web of lies had already begun to fall apart at the seams and her subsequent downfall was imminent.

In 1994, Dena took the final step in her downward spiral of darkness: murder. Detectives believe at this time Julian may have begun to discover the extent of his wife's lies before she took his life with a massive overdose of dothiepin, an anti-depressant, and aspirin hidden in his curry over the course of some days.

Julian loved curry with extra spice, a fact that Dena took advantage of to mask the bitter taste of the poison.

It was on Julian Webb's birthday, June 30th, that his devious wife first informed Julian's mother over the phone that her son had fallen ill and had in fact been sick since Tuesday, two days before.

Dena told his mother that her son had "stayed in the sun too long" and had drunk himself into a stupor, which struck his mother as strange.

She knew that her son didn't partake in alcohol.

Friends and work colleagues of Julian had their suspicions as well, as it was very unlike him to be so sick and to not check in with his loved ones. After his second day of missed work, a male co-worker called to inquire if Julian was okay.

"Oh, well, he's sick," Dena said before hanging up on the man. A number of people called the house inquiring after Julian's health, and each caller would receive a vague, fantastic story as to why he could not come to the phone or work.

At 1:30 a.m. in the morning, on Julian's birthday, Dena would ring the doorbell at the Howell residence, waking them.

She told them that she could not wake up her husband and that he was not breathing. When Dena finally called for help, her husband was long dead and rigid in his bed.

Dena presented the police with two bottles, alleging that her husband had taken an overdose of antidepressants and aspirin on purpose. This was a hard pill for his family to swallow, however, as Julian was a fitness fanatic. He never drank or even took aspirin as he was regimented toward clean living.

"I was awake when the police came 'round to tell me what had happened," Julian's mother recalled. "And I knew as soon as I saw them, before I'd spoken to them, and I heard the police car from upstairs. I just knew."

Julian Webb died of an overdose on his 31st birthday in his bed, at least two hours before an ambulance was called.

Julian's coworkers recall coming up to their work building and finding Dena sitting on the front steps a very short time after his death. She was described as moving between crying and lucidity, and the way she seemed to go between the two so quickly unnerved those that witnessed it. Dena is reported to have said in the same breath, "Julian's dead. I need to speak to someone about the insurance money." To any sane person, these two sentences could not possibly be said in the same conversation, much less the same breath, and yet here was this woman wearing a nightgown and jacket, saying just that.

Dena told the police that her husband committed suicide, but his apparent good health and happy attitude prior to his "sickness" prompted police to investigate. They would discover that the antidepressants belonged not to Julian Webb, but to Dena. Still, the pills were kept in a drawer in the kitchen, where Julian could have easily found and taken them, and thus the fact the pills belonged to Dena held little weight. Though the coroner could not confirm that he had taken the dose accidentally, there was not enough evidence to prove foul play so the medical examiner recorded an open verdict.

Wasting no time, Dena attempted to collect thirty-five thousand pounds from Julian's pension plan which was to be released in the event of his death. Julian's mother would not allow her son's murderer to get away with his life and his money, however, and she was able to quickly establish that Dena was not his next of kin as she was still legally married to her first husband.

Dena also attempted to have Julian's remains cremated, but his family and investigators were able to successfully prevent such an evidence damaging act. It would not be until her trial for attempting to murder her third husband, however, that Julian's body would be exhumed.

The funeral was held at a church on Hayling Island in Northney. Dena Webb showed up wearing a high-riding mini-skirt and a blouse that revealed her ample cleavage.

The right side of the church was packed with friends and family mourning the loss of their Julian, and to the left sat the lone figure of Dena in sexy attire. Friends and colleagues describe Dena's face as emotionless and noticed that the flowers she brought appeared to have been taken from the cemetery nearby.

Much to his family's dismay, Julian's death was eventually ruled an accidental overdose, and Dena Webb moved on in her hunt for a new man to take deadly advantage of.

The freshly widowed Dena looked for love by advertising in the personal ads, describing herself as a "bubbly blonde."

No one proved clever enough to resist her charm. Businessmen, teachers, a prison officer, and even a convicted rapist fell under her ruthless spell before she dumped them or vanished. Detectives believe Dena successfully conned her victims out of a total of a half-million pounds.

One of her victims, Robert Waite, was found and interviewed. He had worked with Dena in 1980 and, years later, suddenly received a card from her inviting him to a reunion party. He called her, and Dena invited him to dinner then seduced him.

Dena would tell Waite that Julian had died from an overdose of steroids and that her first husband, Lee Wyatt, had beaten and attacked her regularly. Waite believed her, as he had no reason not to. But when Mr. Waite began to pull away out of disinterest, Dena quickly convinced him that she was dying of a terminal illness. Wishing to help a dying woman, he promised to take her to one of her favorite places, Florida, to care for her during her last months of life. After they arrived, while the two were lying in bed at a motel, Waite woke to feel a sharp prick in his side. He became entirely sure that Dena drugged him and slept through an entire day.

Soon after, Dena left him for broke, saying she had to appear as a witness in an anti-mafia trial in New York. She was actually flying back to Britain as she was due to appear in court for defrauding the Woolwich. For three weeks, Waite was stranded. Evenually, he came back to England and on August 31st, 1995 he discovered that Dena Webb had just been convicted of fraud and sent to jail. It was revealed during this trial that Dena had falsified the alleged death threats sent to her by mail from Lee Wyatt, and even his recorded calls were scripted by her. At the time of their creation, Lee believed that he was creating them to protect his family. The police were able to conclude that Lee was in fact hundreds of miles away during the time of the thefts working in Newquay under an assumed identity, and the charges against him were dropped. Dena was released after only nine months, and she soon returned home.

A NEW MAN, ANOTHER SUCKER

Richard Thompson was just another name on the long list of pockets Dena wished to empty when he discovered her personal ad in a Lonely Hearts column. The two met and "hit it off", marrying in a Holiday Inn in Florida.

The two were forced to round up strangers, one of which was the manager of the hotel, as witnesses after Dena's supposed "friends and family" did not show.

Thompson had money and owned a home in an affluent community which Dena found to her liking. She lied and charmed Thompson, claiming a love of deep-sea fishing which was his favorite hobby.

Dena told Richard that she had won the lottery and could access the money in the States, and so the loving couple made plans to travel overseas and claim her winnings. After the trip had been finalized, Dena enthralled her new husband with ideas of becoming "a big game ocean skipper" and opening a fishing company.

This inspired Richard to attend classes run by the U.S. Coast Guard. He passed his boating exam, a feat that did not come without a huge amount of hard work. Richard then took an early retirement, and his wife used the money to renovate his cottage in order to rent it out while they were away in Florida building their new life. The new Mrs. Dena Thompson then suggested they combine their financial assets, a suggestion that the blissfully in love Richard saw as a reasonable thing to do. He even made out his will to his wife, giving her power of attorney over his financial affairs. Not long after this, Dena allegedly asked him if their waste disposal unit might be powerful enough to crush bones. A chilling question, to be sure, but a question that Richard thought little about.

Unfortunately for Richard, his wife had a murderous surprise in store for him just one day before the couple were to leave for the States.

On that fateful night, according to Richard's testimony, his wife had promised him a wild round of rough, kinky sex which was something he eagerly accepted.

Before getting ready, Dena locked their German Shepard, Oden, away in another room. She then informed her husband that a man would be coming the following day with a green card for him, which he would then be able to use to go to Florida.

She then started to run a hot bath and told him to "get ready for some fun."

With her husband anticipating something kinky, he allowed Dena to tie up his hands and feet.

"Get ready for a night to remember," she cooed, placing a towel over his face.

Dena then picked up a baseball bat and cracked it over his head. Once then twice for good measure.

Stunned with blood pouring into his eyes, Richard jerked and twisted his body enough to loosen the restraints on his wrists. He sat up but Dena was ready for him.

Grabbing a butcher knife from the night stand beside their bed, she stabbed him in the shoulder. Still dazed from the baseball bat hits to the head, Richard miraculously recovered and pushed Dena away.

Dena slipped on his blood on the floor. Richard seized the advantage, pushing his thumb into her eye. Dena went for the knife again but Richard pushed harder with his thumb.

"I'll put your eye through your head if you don't let go of the knife," Richard warned.

THE AFTERMATH

It would be several days after Richard fought for and won his life that the idea to check his bank accounts would suddenly come to him. A quick call had his accountant checking his assets, and sure enough, it was discovered that Dena, the woman he had grown to love, had cleaned out his bank accounts. She also made inquiries about surrendering his 89,000 pound life insurance policy and put up his house for sale without his knowledge.

"I fell for her personality," Richard said afterward. "I trusted her 100 percent."

Dena was put on trial for attempted murder and fraud, with Richard as the key witness.

She would plead not guilty and her attorney claimed it was Richard who attacked his wife, becoming violent when she told him that Florida had all been a lie, and that Dena had hit him with the bat in self-defense.

The jury fell for Dena's charm as well, acquitting her of attempted murder.

The district attorney would call the case his "the most staggering court verdict I ever had."

Dena was, however, sentenced to three years and nine months at Lewes Crown Court on fifteen counts of fraud, involving thousands of pounds that she stole from her husband Richard, as well as two other lovers. Not only had Richard been nearly murdered without warning, but now he was financially bankrupt and emotionally devastated. During the trial, Dena admitted that her husband was not the only one she had defrauded, and she was convicted to eighteen months in jail for stealing 26,000 pounds from her old employer, the Woolwich building society, by setting up fake accounts. She had also stolen 5,000 pounds from a former boyfriend.

"I had never seen such a miscarriage of justice," Richard said. "It was appalling."

Dissatisfied with the outcome of the trial, the police began an investigation into Dena's past and quickly discovered some disturbingly repetitive facts. They discovered a long train of men left destitute in the wake of the "bubbly blonde" that promised them love and companionship. They also took a second look at the fate of her late husband, Julian Webb, and the cruel lies that sent Lee Wyatt into homelessness for three years. Immediately following their discovery of Julian Webb's death and the investigation into Dena regarding his overdose, investigators reopened the case and exhumed Julian Webb's body for further examination. For six years, Dena Thompson had gotten away with murder, but the attack on her current husband would prove to be her undoing.

Forensic scientists confirmed that antidepressants caused his death, but concluded that the medication was administered over a period of time rather than all at once. This ruled out Dena's original claim of suicide and made it clear that Julian had in fact been poisoned over the course of a week. Scientists were able to prove this by examining his stomach and blood content. The last days of Julian Webb's life would have been horrific. Isolated from his friends and family, Julian would lie dying in his bed, knowing something was wrong but unable to help himself or reach out to others. All the while, Dena nursed him, likely feeding him by hand in what must have appeared to be an act of love and devotion. Instead, this monstrous psychopath was dosing him with still more and more antidepressants and aspirin.

Julian's final moments would have been filled with agony as his body shut down, with Dena's emotionless face being the last thing he would ever see.

Nine years after his untimely demise, Julian Webb's killer would finally be brought to justice. In 2003, Dena Thompson received life, with a minimum of sixteen years, for murder.

FINALLY...

Dena Thompson was a master manipulator of people, with one husband murdered, another almost murdered, and a third on the run and penniless.

The Recorder of London, Michael Hyam, is quoted saying to Mrs. Thompson that her crimes were "utterly ruthless and without any pity. Nothing can excuse you for the wickedness of what you did."

Immediately after the conviction, UK investigators put together a large scale search for any and all of Mrs. Thompson's previous victims with the fear that they had a serial killer on their hands. The search took investigators and Interpol across the length of Europe to Bulgaria, where Dena had been a regular visitor throughout the late 1970s and early 1980s. One Bulgarian boyfriend by the name of Stoyan Kostov was never found, and the fear is that he was an early victim of Dena who was no referred to as the "Black Widow." How did she make her way to Bulgaria?

Dena was an avid gymnast at a young age, although she never chose to compete, and her father, Michael Holmes, was highly involved in the sport. This is allegedly how Mrs. Thompson's Bulgarian connections were made.

Inspector Martyn Underhill felt a certain sense of urgency when searching for Mr. Kostov (last known address: 27 K.D. Avramov Street, Svishtov), but was unable to find the man.

"We cannot rule out the possibility that other partners have been injured in some way," Inspector Underhill said.

Dena visited Bulgaria for several years, with her gymnastics connections said to be her reason. Much mystery hangs over these visits and the still missing Kostov, and it is suggested that Dena's murderous ways began long before she ever met Julian Webb. If Kostov is indeed Dena Thompson's first victim, he could be the only person on earth capable of shedding light on what turned Dena towards a life of crime.

The investigation came to an eventual end, however, when no solid evidence could be found on any murders prior to Julian Webb. Some, including a UK journalist named Adrian Gatton, believe that there is much more to the Bulgarian story than could be found by police. It is suggested that the operation carried out by Interpol and West Yorkshire police was done half-heartedly, as they may never have visited Bulgaria.

There are likely many unnamed men made victims by Dena Thompson's grandiose lies, but they might feel too embarrassed to come forward and identify themselves. It is proven that she stole from a dozen different men, but police believe the number to be much larger. Dena Thompson maintains her innocence, and her most recent appeal against conviction has failed.

In 2007, she was sentenced to a minimum of sixteen years in prison.

GOLD DIGGER VIRGINIA LARZELERE

SAMANTHA RUE

Virginia Larzelere: Incarcerated and spared the electric chair

Mid-afternoon shots rang out in the middle of a suburban dental clinic almost 27 years ago. A frantic call was received by emergency dispatch. The call was made by the wife of the slain dentist yelling down the line for assistance to save her husband's life, following a fatal gunshot wound to the chest.

March 8, 1991 was the day that changed Virginia Larzelere's life forever. The cold-blooded murder of her dentist husband Norman Larzelere sparked off a chain of events that culminated in her lifelong incarceration. Although it could be proven that she never pulled the trigger on her husband, the prosecution successfully argued that she was the mastermind behind the crime. Police investigating the crime scene discovered that as Norman lay dying in a pool of blood he mumbled, "Was that Jason?"

Jason was his son, adopted when he had married Jason's mother.

The investigation would result in a bizarre set of confessions that implicated Virginia Larzelere in the murder for money case. Psychiatric and hearsay evidence pointed to the motive of death to be avarice and a psychopathic manipulation of men throughout her life. Although Virginia's death sentence was commuted to life in 2008, she asserts she is still innocent to this day.

The Crime: Murder at midday, March 8, 1991

The masked killer silently entered through the back door of the dentist's surgery, with a sawed-off shotgun held by his side. His mission was to kill Norman Larzelere, possibly for the life insurance money in some sort of deal with Virginia. The sound of footsteps alarmed Norman as he had not heard anyone enter through the door.

During the trial, Dr Larzelere was reported to have said, "Who's there?" The other occupants of the office at the time were his wife Virginia and the state's witness, Kristen Palmieri who barely looked up when Norman went into the corridor to find out what the disturbance was.

Testimony provided in the first murder hearing alleged that upon seeing a gunman in the shady office corridor, he yelled, "No!" and ran back into the office slamming his office door behind him. The gunman who was in close pursuit was able to pull the trigger once, shattering through the door and hitting the doctor's chest. He subsequently died at the scene from a combination of chest trauma causing a pneumothorax (collapsed lung) and fatal blood loss.

His wife, Virginia, rushed to his side and yelled for someone to call 911. The report from the ambulance dispatcher subsequently reported that Virginia yelled to the 911 dispatcher, "Someone just came in and shot my husband! Somebody shot my husband!"

As Norman's life seeped away, she cradled him, crying. The witness alleged that he asked Virginia, "Where's Jason? Was that Jason?" By the time the police and ambulance had arrived, the gunman had fled, leaving behind a trail of devastation and turmoil. Just as he had sneaked into the clinic without being detected that fateful afternoon, as he was able to leave with none of the witnesses able to positively identify him.

The question, "Was that Jason?" uttered by the dying man, formed the basis of an investigation, where the prosecution's case pinning the murder of Dr Norman Larzelere on Virginia's biological son, Jason.

Betrayal, Lies, Manipulation

Piecing together the various players in this shocking murder for money was the task of Detective Dave Gamell. His first major lead came from the confession of Steve Heidle who had called the detective in May to reveal his hand at disposing of the murder weapon. He claimed that he

A BLACK WIDOW LIKE NO OTHER 57

had been directed by Virginia to clean the weapon in muriatic acid and then bury it in concrete.

Heidle claimed that he was aided in his endeavours by the witness Kristen Palmieri, who like himself, was employed by the slain victim's wife, Virginia Larzelere. Both of them gave statements saying that Virginia had blackmailed them into doing terrible things. Heidle also confessed to knowing about a plan to kill Norman for his life insurance and he alleged that she paid her son Jason $200,000 to kill his adopted father and benefactor.

Heidle, like many others that were unveiled during the investigation, was used as a pawn of Virginia Palmieri to assist in the hiding of evidence. Heidle spent hours with Gamell and provided a lot of useful evidence, not just about disposing the weapons but also about the family dynamics at play that led to the murder being committed by Jason.

According to the state prosecutors, the main motive for killing the well-respected and loved dentist was to bank the payout from Norman's recent increase in life insurance, which had been in place just prior to his untimely death.

Heidle claimed that Virginia had an insatiable appetite for men and money. He also claimed she lived a life filled with drugs and crime all of which made him intimidated to stand up to her. He told Detective Gamell, that if she could get her husband killed in broad daylight, then he feared for his own life if he did not do as instructed. He agreed to hide the evidence and buried the gun deep in the waters of Pellicer Creek.

That same afternoon following Heidle's confession, Kristen Palmieri was called for questioning. She corroborated Heidle's account of the events, telling the detective that she knew that hiding the weapons was wrong. She said that she had never believed that Jason could have been the murderer but subsequently Jason had confessed to her that he had been forced to kill his father at Virginia's behest.

Sure enough, police divers uncovered a plastic container with a rusted shotgun embedded in concrete in Pellicer Creek. In exchange for turning state's witness, Heidle and Palmieri were granted immunity from further prosecution.

Following this significant piece of evidence, Virginia Larzelere was caught and arrested by police the following day. It was said she was attempting to flee from Edgewater with a lot of cash and jewellery in her purse. Detective Gamell had years of experience in homicide investigations and claims he could detect her fake mourning. "I've dealt with a lot of murders and a lot of deaths," Gamell said. "And you know when someone mourns legitimately and when someone's overacting. That's how she seemed."

Gold Digging and Incest: the prosecution's case

As the state's case against Jason and his mother unfolded, it was Heidle's statements to police that provided ample motive for the crime. Heidle claimed that he'd overheard a conversation between Jason and Virginia where she had said that she'd increased the life insurance policy and forged his signature. Dr Larzelere had no suspicions of his wife's dark intentions. Heidle's sworn statement reads, "She said she's [forged] all of Norman's legal documents and it was no big deal." Evidence presented in court revealed that prior to the murder, there had been an increase on the value of the life insurance from $1 million to $2.1 million. Furthermore, a few weeks before the murder, it appeared that his will had been amended to favor his wife. Previously, she was not listed as a sole benefactor.

The trial was a field day for sensationalist journalists who reported on the case. There were many scandalous angles to report. Virginia had already been involved in an embezzlement scheme some years before. Although the charges had been dropped, it was clear that the many people in her life (such as the key witness Heidle) did not like her. It was argued that Virginia was a heartless gold digger who had a long history of manipulating all the men in her life in order to get better resources and status.

While Norman had been dearly loved in Edgewater, it was the belief of many in the small town, that Virginia's arrival in his life was a targeted and calculated move by her. She was a ruthless femme fatale who saw the married dentist as an easy mark. Norman had divorced his wife soon after beginning an affair with Virginia and they married within two months of the divorce being finalized.

Heidle was the key witness and he gave evidence throughout the trial of many instances that implicated Virginia with the murder. Allegations were that Norman Larzelere's life insurance policy and will were forged were denied by Larzelere's defence attorney, Jack Wilkins.

Wilkins was an attorney who loved representing members of the rich party crowd to which Virginia belonged. He claimed that it was great to represent this echelon of drug-taking socialites, as they always paid in cash. Wilkins seemed more like *Breaking Bad's* Saul Goodman, flamboyantly representing drug dealers and winning on minor technicalities.

Wilkins was more a party boy than a lawyer, and while he did have credibility in winning some prominent cases, he lacked the experience to deal with serious forensic evidence. Although he won a prominent civil rights case permitting a small town cinema to sell pornographic movies, he was simply out of his depth in a murder trial.

Virginia's poor choice of lawyer was to seal her fate. Wilkins was a dreadful choice to represent her as he'd admitted, "I'd never done a capital murder case before." During Larzelere's appeal case, evidence was tendered to the court to show that Wilkins had a very serious substance abuse problem, with daily use of vodka, cocaine and methamphetamines. Wilkins did try to turn down the case, but Virginia insisted on retaining him.

The relatively inexperienced and often inebriated Wilkins had to go up against the surgical-like precision of Special Prosecutor Dorothy

Sedgwick's argumentative style. Appointed by the District Attorney, Sedgwick was chosen for her assassin-like instincts to win at all costs. She ran a vicious case against Virginia calling into question the background of the accused.

It was only in the subsequent appeal hearings against the death sentence that many important facts about Virginia's early life were brought to light. Much of the blame for this apparent miscarriage of proper judicial process can be laid at Wilkins' feet. Even Sedgwick was on the record commenting that a decent defence lawyer would have called witnesses to refute some of the state's evidence. Wilkins never sought the opinion of a psychiatrist nor any other expert to take the stand on Virginia's behalf.

The multi-generational level of neglect and sexual misconduct towards children was the key to the prosecution case. Court reports show that under psychiatric questioning, it was clear that as a child growing up, Virginia believed that sexual behavior with family members was the norm. This allowed the prosecutor to paint Virginia as a ruthless killer. In other words, if she was a murderer, being an incestuous murderer made it all the more salacious and perhaps believable to the jury who ultimately convicted her of the murder of Dr Norman Larzelere.

Under Sedgwick's direction, the jury was directed to focus on Virginia's apparently insatiable appetite for men and money as the primary motivation for the murder plot. Sedgwick presented psychiatric evidence to prove that Virginia had a personality disorder which caused her pathological love of money and control.

In the trial, Virginia was successfully portrayed as a manipulative woman with psychopathic tendencies who seduced her son Jason to murder his father, in order to benefit from the life insurance claim. She then used money and blackmail to gain the loyalty of people such as Heidle and Palmieri and her own children.

The state was unable to convict Jason and he was acquitted in 1992 as there was insufficient evidence to place him at the scene of the crime that fateful March day in 1991. However Virginia's guilty verdict and death sentence stayed. It was always clear that she did not murder her husband by her own hand, but suspicions remain as to her collusion due to the circumstantial evidence

How did it come to this?

Virginia grew up in the 1950s in a small town called Lake Wales, 60 miles south of Orlando, Florida. She was the oldest of four daughters all living with their Mom and Dad in a three bedroom bungalow in the working class part of the town. Both of her parents worked in a local juice company called Donald Duck.

Dr Mosman, the psychiatrist giving evidence in the appeal case told the court that she had confided to him that her father, "Pee-Wee" Antley, was a strong dictator whose moods ruled the house of women. It was noted he was a huge drinker who sexually abused each of his daughters (and subsequently Virginia's own children Jessica and Jason). In an interview with the Miami New Times in 2013, Virginia said, "sexual abuse doesn't only happen in poor households, does it?"

Virginia's younger sister, Peggy, testified that Virginia took more of the sexual abuse from their father in an attempt to spare her younger sisters. The abuse would gave birth to a burden of silence, of not being able to confide in people outside the family or to get any help for them or their mother. Mosman revealed to the court that the father was, "a chronic alcoholic, sitting on the porch drinking daily, with no outside hobby or social interests."

Virginia left home at the age of seventeen but the scars of abuse never left. Having been a victim of abuse from as young as the age of three, the emotional and sexual trauma stayed with her and influenced her outlook on life and on men. Virginia knew that the best way to survive was to use men to gain access to the wealth that she needed to feel free from her demons.

Her success at attracting many men (she was married three times by the time she was in her early 30s) came about because she was able to use her looks and sexual conduct to acquire goods and status throughout her life. Even Virginia's daughter Jessica (from her first marriage to Harry Mathis), said that the child abuse she had suffered led her to be ruthless and impulsive. Jessica has stated in an interview some years ago that, 'My mother is a very intelligent woman, who had looks which she used to her advantage." The state's case relied on this aspect of her love of the high life and of sexual promiscuity to draw the sketch of her as a ruthless gold-digging murderer.

The entire prosecution case was based on Heidle's voluntary testimony, which painted Virginia as the product of a dysfunctional and incestuous family. It was alleged that her exposure to serious childhood abuse and trauma led to her manipulative and ruthless tendencies. However, no psychiatrist was ever called by the defence to undertake an evaluation of her mental state.

Virginia's teen marriage

In Lake Wales where Virginia was growing up, she did not have any friends. This is because her domineering father felt the need to protect his filthy secret from authorities so visitors were restricted from visiting the home.

Virginia attended and graduated from Lake Wales High school and immediately fled home to marry Harry Mathis when she was only 17 years old. Soon after the marriage, she fell pregnant with Jason and then Jessica. Experts say that people often people who have dysfunctional parents often choose dysfunctional partners, and this certainly appears to be the case with Virginia.

She was trapped as a young mom, from a dysfunctional background now living with an abusive husband. Harry Mathis beat his wife and son Jason, as evidenced in the police records. Virginia divorced him in 1978, determined to be as far away from his abuse as possible, and wanting a new life for her two young children, Jason and Jessica. Instead of seeing her getting away from Harry as a triumph against abuse, the prosecutor used this to demonstrate that Virginia 'burned through' husbands. The prosecutor even used the fact that she wished for her abusive ex-huband's death as evidence of her murderous intent for Norman.

However, despite the various setbacks, abuse and domestic violence there remained in Virginia evidence of a clear determination to not only survive but thrive. Once she had escaped her parental home of horror, she went into another dysfunctional marriage for a brief period. It is also a fact that she had turned to substances to numb the emotional pain from a young lifetime of abuse. She was clearly not the most stable woman in Edgewater, but she was a survivor.

Leaving Mathis started her love of freedom, and of the partying good life that has been portrayed through documentaries about the case.

Socialite in the making

Having been divorced at the age of 25, and with two young children in tow, Virginia was clearly on a mission to find a man that would replace their biological father as a role model in her life. Being denied a good role model of appropriate masculinity, she was easily distracted by the promises of various men simply looking for a woman to bed. However, she was also hungry for money and status but preferred freedom to being tied to a man It appears that her main goal since leaving home at 17 had been to free herself from the control of a man.

Her hunger for a better life, even being married three times before she was 32, demonstrates a decision to turn away from the cycle of abuse that her mother had endured. Virginia's mother stayed by her husband's side through the mistreatment and abuse of all of his daughters. In a sense, her mother colluded with him by permitting the abuse to be perpetuated, child after child. Her misplaced loyalty for, and fear of, her husband kept her at his side.

Virginia's drive to be different from her passive mother showed her adventurous spirit, her impulsiveness and her keen business sense. By the mid-1980's she had worked her way up to being the president of a construction company based in the little town of Edgewater, a seaside town, two hours north of her hometown, Lake Wales. Although Edgewater was still a very small and isolated town, she had successfully changed her fortunes. Her financial success had become like a drug It made her feel good, and the more she did of it, the better she felt.

Her stars changed completely in 1985 due to the happenstance of a dental appointment where she was to meet the love of her life. It was in Dr Norman Larzelere's dental surgery that love was born. Virginia claims that from that first meeting she knew he was 'the one'. The feelings were clearly mutual, as the already married dentist quickly divorced his wife so that he could make a life for Virginia and her children. He embraced Jason and Jessica as his own and officially adopted them when they married.

"There was nothing but love in that household," fhe family's housekeeper Juanita Washington said. "Nothing but love." Upon their marriage, the newlyweds Virginia and Norman promptly moved into a mansion in a prestigious uptown area. The home had previously housed all sorts of people from the higher echelons of society including congressional representatives and bank presidents. By all accounts, despite the differences in their social standings and backgrounds, they seemed to be deliriously happy and to be true soul mates.

Storm clouds over paradise

However, things started to get a bit difficult the following year as Virginia's business went bankrupt amid allegations of embezzlement. Settling out of court, all criminal charges were dismissed. Around this time, her teenage son Jason was getting a bit out of hand, as teenagers in blended families often do.

Jason was a known party boy in the local Orlando gay club scene. He also befriended drag queens and seemed to have inherited his biological father's love of beating women. "He threw me down the stairs and broke my ribs by kicking me over and over again," his sister Jessica recalled. "I had told my dad that Mom was cheating on him with a patient of his." Jason staunchly defended his mother and allegations of her sexual appetites together with her son's strong filial devotion was a source of gossip surrounding their potentially incestuous relationship.

Virginia never denied her sexual liaisons with several men, two of whom testified that she had asked them to 'get rid' of Norman. It was clear that whatever their relationship was in public, Norman was unable to control his headstrong and hard-partying wife. Some of the testimonies only came to light when these men of low character asked to be paid to testify, making them barely credible.

No friends to testify on Virginia's behalf

With the public salivating upon every salacious fact, it was fair to say that Virginia and Jason Larzelere were convicted in the court of public opinion before the jury delivered its 5-7 guilty verdict for Virginia. Jason was subsequently acquitted due to the flimsy evidence by a disgruntled employee (Heidle) being the sole evidence in the case. Subsequent hearings brought to light the fact that the lone gunman that fateful day was not Jason, as Heidle had conveniently framed him for the murder. As Heidle had been given immunity from prosecution, many speculate that he tainted the stories about Virginia to protect himself and that it was he who murdered Larzelere. He committed suicide in 1999.

The allegations that Virginia was the mastermind who had her husband killed in cold blood to collect on his significant life insurance were presented but never successfully refuted. Her defence lawyer did not call any witness to the stand to testify on her behalf. A lifetime of alienation from meaningful relationships robbed her of this comfort. Her childhood of abuse and neglect impaired her ability to make and sustain meaningful and enduring friendships.

Her death sentence was overturned in 2008 though she remains incarcerated in the Homestead Correctional Institution, a 65-year-old widow, and she still maintains her innocence.

BLACK WIDOW BETTY LOU BEETS

ALICE WATERS

Betty Lou Beets is a perfect historical example of how multifaceted crime can be, how a victim could become an aggressor, or an aggressor may adopt the mask of victimhood, and how all is not necessarily as it seems. Convicted for murdering two men and assaulting or attempting to kill four, Betty Lou's story is one that would send chills down the spine of any man from any era. Only the fourth woman to be executed for murder, despite the overall statistics hovering around forty to fifty cases of capital punishment per year, her crimes were too gruesome and cold for the court to offer her a lesser sentence... or were they? As we shall see when we delve into her history, despite Betty Lou's extensive criminal record and constant charges against her from ex husbands and her own children, the justice system was eager to give her a way out of the death sentence and allow her to live her natural life out in prison. And although there were some mitigating circumstances, it is telling that Betty Lou Beets almost got away with a life sentence in a situation where many others would have been executed without remorse.

Betty Lou Beets was born Betty Lou Dunevant on the 12th of March 1937, in Roxboro, North Carolina, USA. Her parents were initially tobacco farmers, whose main pleasure in life was alcohol, resulting in rampant alcoholism and a violent family life not atypical of the rural poor of the Great Depression. They lived on a diet of salt pork and various flours, barely touching vegetables or fruit, let alone eggs, fish, nuts or pulses, essential for developing a healthy brain and body. Furthermore, Betty Lou was disabled. She was not completely deaf, but hard of hearing due to having contracted the measles some time between the ages of three and six. Her fever was so severe and prolonged that she suffered damage to her brain and ears. As her hearing was affected at such a young age, she suffered an impairment to her speech similar to what many deaf or hard of hearing children suffer. At another time, or in another family, Betty Lou may have received treatment and hearing aids, but as a poor family in 1940, they could not afford to get her the treatment she would have needed to hear and speak normally. Her education was strongly impacted as she could not learn to read or study, resulting in borderline illiteracy and innumeracy and a frustrating life at home and away. Betty Lou also claimed she had been raped by her father in early childhood, as well as sexually abused by others. By the age of twelve her family life was falling apart. Her mother had been institutionalized due to breakdowns caused by alcoholism and Betty Lou had to drop out of school so she could care for her younger brother and sister. Her father, who seemed to see her as a surrogate mother for her siblings, became guarded against any sign of Betty Lou escaping and would beat her for not taking full responsibility for her siblings. She was often at the doctor's office or in hospital for the injuries he inflicted on her. She finally left school completely. The family moved to Hampton, Virginia, while Betty Lou was still a young girl, so that her father could work as a machinist. They were poor, she was young and disabled and she was a victim at the hands of the very people who were supposed to care for her. These circumstances were hardly the healthiest for the young girl to grow up in, and it is not shocking that Betty Lou became increasingly unstable and inclined to criminality in such an environment during such a time of deprivation. However it is also noteworthy that many more people suffered equal or worse hardship, yet did not turn to criminal activity. Perhaps it was the combination of everything, all together at once, but as she grew up something was going very, very wrong inside Betty Lou.

At the age of fifteen she married her first husband, Robert Franklin Branson. Far from an age where anyone feels quite ready to move into adulthood, Betty Lou was married for the first time. She would remain with him for seventeen years before finally divorcing. Although she levied accusations of violence against all her husbands, Robert Franklin Branson was the only one whose life she did not threaten directly herself. It appears he picked up where her father left off. If she was ever a unilateral victim, this may have been the one time. Within the first year she attempted suicide and became pregnant. They had a daughter together. She also later had a son with Robert Branson, who was also named Robert after his father. They went onto have four more children. Their children may have been a factor in reducing the marital violence, extending the duration of the relationship and, ultimately, saving Robert Branson Senior's life. In 1958 he evicted her from their home and put her on a bus to Virginia while he kept her children, at which point Betty again attempted suicide via an overdose of sleeping pills. They divorced in 1969, which left Betty Lou a financial and emotional wreck.

Being single took its toll on Betty Lou. She attached her self-worth to her ability to stay married. She began drinking to fight her feelings of loneliness. Between her own insecurities and the hard time she had getting money from either Robert Branson or the Welfare service to support her, Betty Lou soon felt she needed to remarry. She married Billy York Lane at the age of thirty two. Their marriage was a tumultuous one, and very short. There was evidence of mutual violence and disregard for each other's wellbeing. Lane had been abusive towards a previous partner and Betty Lou responded to his violence in turn. Her daughters recall how he used to beat her senseless and how she used to attack him. He initially wanted to charge her for attempted murder, but swiftly dropped the charges after he was forced to admit he had attacked her, broken her nose and threatened her life. They divorced the same year and remarried again shortly after the trial.

After Betty Lou shot at him, Billy York Lane divorced her again, only a month after their remarriage, this time for good. It would prove the wisest decision of his life, as her subsequent husbands found out.

Betty Lou remained single for a year and unmarried for eight more years. During the interim Betty Lou worked in a warehouse, then took up work at a topless bar to cover the bills. She sent two of their children back home to Branson, as she could not afford to care for them. She went on to marry Ronnie C. Threlkold, her boyfriend of seven years, at the age of forty. However this relationship would be as unpredictable, violent and dangerous for Ronnie as it was for Billy. In this case there was little evidence Ronnie had been violent towards Betty Lou, although she accused him of violence at later dates, but her habits had been firmly cemented and she continued to display abusive behaviour towards him. She also continued to work at the topless bar, resulting in arrests and thirty days in country jail under the charge of public lewdness. Despite their seven year courtship, the marriage lasted just a year, culminating in Betty Lou Beets's attempted homicide of Ronnie in 1978, where she shot him in the stomach, wounding him, and their divorce in 1979.

She married Doyle Wayne Barker at the age of forty one, closely after her divorce from Threlkold. Their marriage lasted a mere seven weeks before her violent behaviour drove Doyle away from her. However his own violence was undeniable. He had stalked her, assaulted her and raped her during their short relationship. The day he left Betty Lou had bruises all over her face, neck, arms and chest. There is no available record of the divorce, however all living parties assumed it had taken place. However Doyle Wayne did not get out of their marriage unscathed. He disappeared after their divorce and his body was found years later, buried under a garage, killed by three gunshots.

But this grisly deed was not uncovered for many more years to come. Rather, Betty Lou went on to marry a firefighter named Jimmy Don Beets, her final husband, at the age of forty four.

"Jimmy Don Beets was a wonderful man," said a family friend. "He was loved by so many people. An old country boy that a lot people had respect for."

Their courtship would last a mere six months. Betty Lou would meet Jimmy while she worked as a waitress and the seduction began. Her two sons moved in with them. This would be her final marriage, and her actions within it would be her undoing. Although their courtship had been pleasant, they both suffered from alcoholism, which slowly drove their marriage to the same violence she had experienced previously. Less than a year later she murdered him by gunshot, and this time she was caught. Robert Branson, her son from her first marriage, had been informed that she intended to kill her last husband, telling him to steer clear of the residence as the murder took place. On the 6th of August 1983, Robert Branson Junior left their home and Betty Lou Beets committed the gruesome act. Not only did Robert provide evidence that the act was premeditated, but he also was expected to participate. Two hours after leaving the house, Robert Branson Junior returned, finding his step father dead with two gunshot wounds in his body. Rather than seek assistance, Robert Branson Junior, either tainted by a lifetime with a mother who viewed abuse and murder as daily events or himself an individual with low empathy, helped his mother to dispose of the body. Betty Lou Beets and Robert Branson Junior carted Jimmy Don Beets' body outside to an ornamental wishing well that stood in the front yard of their house. Undetected, they cast the body inside.

Then, Betty Lou returned to the house to cover up her acts. She called the police to report her husband missing from their Cedar Creek Lake home. The next day, Betty Lou became more devious. Perhaps inspired, perhaps unnerved by her success killing Doyle Wayne Barker, she realized she needed to create a story with which to divert the police from her trail. Robert Branson Junior recalled to the press how she had taken some of Jimmy Don Beets's heart medication down to his boat at the lake. Then she had removed the propeller, placed the medication in the boat and abandoned it, floating loosely in the water. Later that day, as the twenty four hours since Jimmy Don Beets's initial disappearance drew to a close, various officials began the search for the presumably missing man. Officers from the Henderson County Sheriff's department, various members of the fire department, as well as agents from the Texas Parks and Wildlife department searched for three weeks. They naturally found no body. However they did find Jimmy Don Beets's boat drifting in the lake, near to the Redwood Beach Marina. There they found his fishing license, an unused life jacket and the heart medication which Betty Lou Beets had placed there. Not knowing anything about the murder or the forged evidence, they brought Betty Lou Beets to the Marina as the sole witness, where she identified the boat and its contents as those of her husband. Although no body had been recovered, it was considered case closed.

Betty Lou Beets would have likely got away with both murders, were it not for confidential information given to the Henderson County Sheriff's Department two years later. The information suggested that Jimmy Don Beets had not disappeared innocently, and that his assumed death, with no body that had been found, may be the result of foul play. The evidence was enough that the cold case was reopened in Spring 1985. As their suspicions became stronger, the investigators were drawn to Betty Lou Beets, who was arrested on the 8th of June of 1985 and then booked into the Henderson County Jail. An officer on the case, Rick Rose, who had been in charge of her arrest warrant, secured a further warrant to search the Beets's home and lands, including the yard. Ultimately, they discovered Jimmy Don Beets's remains buried under the wishing well where he had been left two years prior. But another discovery would surface that would further disturb the case. Also in the back yard was a storage shed which could be moved. When the officers moved it, something compelled them to disturb the soil that had lain there several years. Perhaps it was some confidential evidence or perhaps it was just intuition, but it paid off when they discovered a second body. Doyle Wayne Barker, still missing, was buried there, with three bullets in his body. All five bullets matched the .38 caliber pistol which had been seized from their home after another incident of Betty Lou's violent outbursts. Thanks to the calls she had made the very day of his disappearance there was no room to argue that she had been abusing drugs or alcohol at the time, but there had been no physical evidence that suggested to detectives at the time that Jimmy Don had been abusing her when the incident took place. Her position was weak.

Faced with the evidence, Robert Branson Junior and his sister Shirley finally confessed to their awareness of the killings, as well as their hand in the crimes that had taken place. Not only had Betty Lou told her son about the murder, but she had also informed her daughter, by the Shirley Stegner and not living at the family home, that she planned on killing her husband. Shirley was motivated by her confession to also confess to her involvement in another crime. She told the detectives that she had been involved in the burial of Doyle Wayne Barker's body in October of 1981 after Betty Lou had shot him to death.

In an effort to make herself more likeable to the jury, Betty Lou Beets raised her history of domestic violence as an excuse for her violent behaviour, levying charges against all her prior husbands, as well as her father. However, this would be the first that anyone had heard of most of these charges. This may have been due to attitudes of the times, a desire to protect her children, or the apparently two-sided nature of most of these incidents, however the jury would not believe her claims. They were just too convenient. Instead, it was clear to them that Betty Lou Beets was an unstable and dangerous woman and the only connection between the five men she married and their violence. Whatever the situation was, her psychological well being was never considered during the trial. Despite the obvious impact her upbringing and life would have on her mental state and the fact that her actions up until that point were indicative of definite mental illness, the trial system of the time did not account for that.

Furthermore, the premeditated nature of her actions was evident through her children's abundant testimonials, where they confessed she had shared her intent to kill not only the husbands she managed to murder, but that she had expressed a desire to kill all the men she had been married to. Not only that, but her success concealing the bodies, under the wishing well and under the garden shed, showed a lack of remorse and serious consideration of her crimes. However it seems Betty Lou had not been as careful as she thought. As soon as the trial began, various other witnesses emerged to testify against her. Various people recalled her attempting to collect life insurance of over a hundred thousand dollars as well as a pension of over a thousand dollars a month after Jimmy Don's declared death. A year after the official death of Jimmy Don Beets, she successfully sold his boat, the primary evidence that he had disappeared. She claimed she did not know about his pension or insurance, however seeing as Jimmy Don Beets was already retired and claiming his pension, this claim fell short. Furthermore, had she no awareness of them she would not have pursued either so actively. She claimed she had been told about them when she visited an attorney by the name or E. Ray Andrews about a fire insurance claim she needed to make, at which point he discovered she could claim his insurance and pension. However her own filing for these benefits did not align with the supposed visit, and the only person who could say for sure that she had not known about her deceased husband's finances was E. Ray Andrews himself, who agreed to represent her in exchange for the rights to book and movie deals concerning her life and case.

Betty Lou Beets was indicted for murder for remuneration or the promise of remuneration, with her recovery of his life insurance and pension as evidence. She plead not guilty and was taken to trial, where she was found guilty of the capital offence of first degree murder on the 11th of October of 1985. She was found again guilty during a hearing on the 14th of October 1985 and was sentenced to death by the trial court. This was due to her prior history of violence and attempted murders, which suggested that she would present a threat to others in the future, specifically to any man who entered a relationship with her again. Yet her conviction and sentence were quickly and successfully appealed to the Texas Court of Criminal Appeals. Such was the situation that, under Texas law, crime for the sake of insurance and pension claims was not covered by the definition of "murder for remuneration", instead falling into two separate categories of first degree murder and insurance fraud, or crime with intent to commit insurance fraud. The Texas Court of Criminal Appeals reversed her conviction for capital murder, citing the Texas Penal Code as evidence that her particular case could not be filed as "murder for remuneration". The State then requested a rehearing of the cause. Although her original conviction had been overturned, the fact remained that Betty Lou Beets was guilty of homicide under some circumstance or another.

On the 21st of September of 1988, the Court of Criminal Appeals reinstated her conviction and sentence based on the evidence received. Betty Lou Beets was on death row. Her execution was scheduled for the 8th of November 1989.

However her court case did not go as it should have in the first place. Attorney E. Ray Andrews was heavily invested in sensationalizing her case as much as he could, seeing as he would profit enormously from the case blowing up into a media phenomenon. So although she claimed and he later agreed that she had known nothing of her husband's finances, the trial was conducted under the assumption that she was fully aware of the money she would receive. Not only that, but E. Ray Andrews did everything in his power to create a more dramatic case on both sides, which ultimately meant excluding Betty Lou from much of the information about her own trial. Betty Lou was becoming desperate at this point. Although she had a long history of domestic violence, attempted murder and two bodies in her garden, she decided to attempt to blame the murder of Jimmy Don Beets on Robert Branson Junior, her own son. She did not seem to have made the statement in sound mind, but E. Ray Andrews allowed her to speak on her own behalf and did not retract it, as it added dramatic quality to the event. He tried to cover up later, saying that Betty Lou had possibly been taking the blame for her son, however he had no proof other than that Robert Branson Junior was male and from a rough background. This statement and its acceptance horrified the court, as it was alarming to them to see a mother who, rather than protect her children, was willing to throw them under the bus by falsely accusing them of a crime she had more than evidently committed. Furthermore, by admitting and adhering to the story that Robert Branson Junior was in fact the actual killer, Betty Lou lost all chances of arguing that she acted in self-defence and made her own accusations of domestic violence against Jimmy Don and her prior husbands completely irrelevant. This is despite the fact that a leading domestic violence specialist of the time believed Betty Lou Beets had been significantly mentally impacted by her experiences, and that she suffered "the emotional, cognitive, and behavioural components of battered woman syndrome, rape trauma syndrome, and PTSD" which he added must have interacted with her pre-existing organic brain damage from her childhood illness, history of battering and substance abuse. All together, this would have presented a robust case for her mental illness and need for treatment rather than punishment. However E. Ray Andrews discarded this option in favour of the more dramatic choice of supporting Betty Lou's accusation against her son. They became stuck in the position of having to argue she did not kill her husband at all. This context may have reduced her sentence, or made her eligible to claim insanity. However neither of these options were available.

Throughout the entire case, E. Ray Andrews failed to represent her seriously and did nothing to prevent her from shooting herself in the foot repeatedly. In fact, seeing the case was a lost cause and that he stood to gain more from her sentence than her freedom, Andrews began drinking heavily for the duration of the trial. He chose not to bear witness to her claims that she did not know about Jimmy Don Beets's pension or insurance, which would have transformed the case to one of murder in the context of domestic violence, rather than murder for remuneration. He managed to offer the jury no reasons to consider that Betty Lou was not a serious threat to those around her, eventually sealing her fate. Yet he remained her attorney for the duration of her appeal as well. It was he who raised the point that her financial gain was not necessarily the motivator for murder, but a by product. He also finally raised that she was not aware of the insurance or pension until she spoke to him, however this was met with scepticism due to his negligence to mention it any sooner, and was perceived as a lie in effort to overturn Betty Lou's criminal charges after his initial failure to protect her.

On the 16th of October 1989, Betty Lou filed a motion called a stay of execution which would delay her execution to give her time to prepare and file a habeas corpus application with the state. On the 1st of November she filed the application and the trial court delayed her execution so that the claims she was raising, such as consideration towards her mental state and marital conditions, could be properly addressed. During this time Betty Lou wrote several letters from prison in which she attempted to defend her good name and that of her last husband. She attempted to balance the accusations that she was a black widow by reminding the court that she was Jimmy Don's fourth wife as well. However his previous wives did not come forward to support her. She also defended her own identity, denying that she ever worked as a barmaid, regardless of her own charges for lewd behaviour, and that she was never on welfare, despite her claims after her first divorce. She also said that the Fire Department Chaplain, who stated he had informed her about Beets's insurance and pension, had spoken to her sister in law, Betty Beets, instead. She even quibbled over the descriptions of her garden, insisting the well was a planter in the shape of a well and not an actual well. It was clear that Betty Lou Beets was desperate to save face and project a more pleasant, more ordinary identity than the one which E. Ray Andrews had created for her in the courtroom. It was also clear that her mental health was degrading as she endured life in prison and submitted her habeas corpus petition. In her petition she argued against her sentence of the death penalty, raising issues such as the alleged value Jimmy Don Beets apparently added the community, the testimonials of victims and sufferers whose statements were unconstitutional under the Victim Impact Statements act of 1987, and the poor assistance which E. Ray Andrews provided, especially regarding her history of domestic abuse. Yet without his help in writing and presenting the letter, her claims were weak and not fully backed by legal evidence. Andrews did not visit her from the point of her sentencing and prepared for her trials without ever speaking to her. Furthermore, she could have claimed that his services were provided against American Bar Association rules, which prohibit the trade of legal services for copyright issues, such as the rights to her case. None of this was raised by her against him, and as such it was not considered during her habeas corpus appeal.

However on the 27th of June her appeal for state habeas corpus was turned away. She was placed in the position of proving that, had E. Ray Andrews presented a testimony about her lack of awareness of the insurance and her history of domestic violence, the jury would have judged her not guilty of a capital crime. Without a proper attorney to defend her, it would be impossible for Betty Lou to prove this was the case, and the court deemed Andrews's mistakes to have been harmless to her trial. The Fifth Circuit Court of Appeals went on to turn down her final appeals. The judges remained convinced that, regardless of any remaining evidence, Betty Lou Beets's history of violence and attempted murder, along with the two concealed bodies in her garden, were evidence enough that a death sentence was a fair response to the crime that had taken place. She had displayed violence her whole life, even towards men who had not presented a threat to her, and had attempted to kill all but one of her husbands. She had concealed her murders carefully and for many years and was willing to place the blame on her own adult son. In other words, regardless of her own situation, her criminal intent was viewed as evident and incorrigible, and her death sentence was the only fitting end to her crime spree.

On death row, Betty Lou Beets retained some supporters, mostly her own children. Some of Betty Lou's daughters went to E. Ray Andrews with photographic evidence of the domestic abuse she had suffered in order to request a parole review, but were declined. They insisted on presenting the evidence that she had suffered and that her acts of violence were a result of brain damage and abuse, not of malicious intent. Faye Lane, one of her daughters, insisted that her mother would only have done anything so horrific if she believed she was abused. Domestic violence awareness groups and charities acting against the death sentence appealed to have her sentence changed to a life sentence in prison, based not only on her own suffering, but on their universal stance against the irreversible process of the death penalty. Yet even those defending her maintained that she was a violent, unpredictable woman and not safe to exit into the general public.

And not all her children were so kind. Shirley told the press that Doyle Wayne Barker was killed because he owned the trailer where they lived, and that after the divorce which Barker had initiated, Betty Lou and her children would be evicted from the trailer and left homeless. This set a precedent where even her own daughter could not believe that Betty Lou was completely unaware of the financial benefits of murdering Jimmy Don Beets, especially not after she had successfully killed Barker. Knowing that she was still doubted and seeing hope as ever distant, Betty Lou composed her memoirs from death row, presenting her case.

Beets turned to her last resort which was to appeal to then-governor George W. Bush to spare her life. After a media incident where he jokingly insulted the last woman to be executed in Texas in an insensitive manner, George W. Bush seemed keen to prove he had no bias against women, even in the prison system, and agreed to review her case. This would have meant hearing the witnesses which had not been heard by the trial lawyer and present a case against her execution based on the circumstances of her life, including medical and psychiatric evidence. He could have granted her a thirty day reprieve in which he made his decision, however this never materialized. His number was made available and he received thousands of calls and letters from people urging him to spare her, with only fifty seven endorsing her sentence. Yet he did not grant the reprieve or halt the execution.

Betty Lou Beets was finally executed on the 24th of February of 2000, via lethal injection. Protestors from various organisations gathered outside as her sentence awaited. She declined both her last meal and her final statement, having been given by then enough time to make sense of what was happening and to say everything which needed to be said. Strapped to the death chamber gurney, she received her injection at six pm and died within eighteen minutes. She was sixty two years old. She left behind five adult children, nine grandchildren and six great-grandchildren, as well as her memoirs. Her story may be shocking, and it may be hard to pick sides at times, but that is exactly why her trial presents a solid case against the black and white ideals the court system held regarding crime and punishment, perpetrator and victim, defence and offence. Someone can at once be a victim of horrific crimes and a perpetrator of them, at once be a defendant and raise accusations, at once deserve punishment yet suffer a crime gone unpunished. There is no doubt that Betty Lou Beets was a violent woman who invited violence into her own life, an alcoholic and a murderer. However there is no doubt either that she was a good mother within her capacity, a victim of a series of horrific crimes, a disabled person with a background she could not escape and a desperate woman who saw no way out of her situation. Neither black nor white, good not bad, Betty Lou Beets sits in the grey areas of the law.

BLACK WIDOW JANIE LOU GIBBS

JANE CARLISLE

Janie Lou Hickox was born on December 25th, Christmas day, 1932 in Cordele, Georgia. Cordele is now a town with just over 11 000 residents, and is proudly known as the Watermelon Capital of the World. The city is named after Cordelia Hawkins who was the eldest daughter of Colonel Samuel Hawkins, the president of the Savannah, Americus and Montgomery Railway. In November of 1864, the area temporarily served as the capital of Georgia, but Cordele as it is now knows was founded in 1888 as a junction between two major railroads: the Savannah, Americus and Montgomery line and the Georgia Southern and Florida. Notable people from the area include jazz and blues singers, sportsmen, a White House Press Secretary and the president of an international Christian TV network. Nobody suspected that a serial killer who would be a black widow was growing up in their midst.

There is not much information about Janie's upbringing, but it was strictly religious and she grew up in a fairly poor family. Janie was married to Charles Clayton Gibbs, a farmer, when she was only fifteen. The two moved to the nearby town of Arabi which was just under ten miles away from Cordele, a mere fifteen minutes by car. Both of these towns fall under the Crisp County district. Arabi now has a population of 586, with 185 hosueholds and 125 families living in the town. Janie and Charles were regular churchgoers, and they had three boys: Roger Ludean Gibbs, Melvin Watess Gibbs, and Marvin Ronald Gibbs. For eighteen years, they lived quiet and devoted lives on the farm until tragedy began to take blow after blow upon the family.

Janie was known for spending all of her spare time helping out at the church and for her day-care service that she ran in her home for children of working mothers. Accounts note that on most days Janie would have around twenty-five children at her house aside from her own sons. While some believed her to have almost fanatic religious beliefs, all members of Janie's church and community believed her to be sound of mind and to know the difference between right and wrong, testimonies that they would later make in the investigation. Nobody felt that Janie had any emotional or mental issues, and simply knew her as a devoted mother who held God and the church close to her heart. When she wasn't looking after children in the community, Janie was helping out with events around the church and other ways to support the congregation.

Just before the tragedies began to occur, Janie had travelled to Albany, Georgia for a doctor's appointment. There she had been diagnosed with Lou Gehrig's disease, a motor neurone disease that destroys muscle control, is also known as amyotrophic lateral sclerosis or ALS. The disease progresses from a stiffness of muscles to twitching while the person becomes increasingly weaker. Eventually, once their muscles have decreased in size enough, the patient has trouble with speaking, swallowing, and eventually breathing. Janie was very aware that her body would begin to systematically shut itself down. After her trial, her defense lawyer Frank Martin stated that this was one of the most tragic aspects of the case as far as he was concerned. Frank believed that due to Janie's acute awareness of how her illness would progress paired with her fanatic religious beliefs, she wanted everybody that was close to her in the world to go to heaven so that she would be with them when she finally passed. Although Janie never admitted this in court, the murder of her husband, three sons, and grandson, all of whom she loved dearly, suggests that this might have been a contributing factor to the decisions or delirium that ended in her intentionally poisoning five members of her family.

The first member of the family to go was her husband, Charles Clayton Gibbs, who died on the 21st January 1966 when he was only thirty-nine years old. Janie was an avid cook, and she always had home cooked meals ready for her family when they returned home from work or school. After having had one such meal, Charles collapsed in the family home and was taken to hospital. Janie went to the hospital to care for him and brought a flask of soup with her. After Charles was served this final meal, he died painfully from stomach cramps and convulsions. Years later, investigators realized that this soup must have been laced with a particularly strong dose of arsenic from rat poison that Janie had been giving him in trace amount in his meals and coffees.

When administered in small amounts like this, it can be very difficult to determine if somebody is a victim of arsenic poisoning unless a doctor thinks to specifically check for it. Arsenic poisoning can result in a host of different symptoms and organ failures, so it is often the case that medical professionals are waiting for more evidence to be able to provide a solid diagnosis while the victim continues to be poisoned by somebody close to them. Symptoms can include abdominal pain and cramping, diarrhea, vomiting, dark urine, dehydration, vertigo, delirium, shock, hair loss, and convulsions. Arsenic is flavorless and odorless, making it very difficult for somebody to connect their normal food and beverage consumption with their illness. Arsenic poisoning can affect the skin, liver, lungs, and kidneys, which is both why it is such a potentially fatal condition and why it is difficult to detect without a hunch. In the case of Charles, his death was written down to an undiagnosed liver disease that he had been suffering for some time. While the doctors wanted to perform an autopsy on her husband to be sure, Janie said that she didn't want him 'all cut up', and her wishes were respected.

The church community provided an overwhelming amount of support for the Gibbs family once Charles had passed. The entire congregation was shocked, Charles having seemed to be in such good health until recent times, and also because he was still so young. The Gibbs family were provided with company, meals, emotional support, and everything that the members of their church community could possibly extend. When the life insurance claim for Charles came through, Janie donated a significant portion of these funds to the church to demonstrate her thanks for everything that they had done and her belief in the community. Janie claimed that she and the boys would have to continue on as best they could, and that she felt that with the strength of the church community behind them they would be able to make it through. Even after their home burned down soon after Charles' death and the family moved back to Janie's home town of Cordele, Janie continued to offer day-care services for the children of working mothers. There has never been an investigation into the house burning down, but the timing is certainly curious. Is it possible that Janie felt this was the only way to justify moving her family back to her home town of Cordele? It is clear from the rest of her actions over this two year period that she wasn't thinking rationally, and perhaps she wanted to escape the physical environment where she had been married for all of those years. Whatever the reason, just as nobody suspected that Janie had anything to do with the death of her husband, there was no investigation into whether or not the house burned down due to arson.

It was around this time that the oldest Gibbs son Roger took notice of a girl in their congregation, Ellen Penny. A relationship began to blossom between them under the watchful eye of Janie. The two teenagers began to spend more and more time together at church events, and participated in the same activities together. If Roger was assigned the duty of retrieving the bibles at the end of a ceremony, Ellen would always be there too help him. Very soon the two began to date. Over the next year Roger and Ellen married and she became pregnant with their first child. Ellen began living at the Gibb's residence, but this relationship and pregnancy was against a dark backdrop. It is difficult to say whether Janie took an immediate dislike to Ellen, or whether she did not want her son getting married and having a child so early like she had herself. Perhaps she wanted a different life for him, or harbored some resentment on being married off at such a young age. Either way, Janie never had a good relationship with Ellen and many times would behave as if she almost didn't register her existence.

Only months after Charles' death, Marvin began to develop the same symptoms as his father had. Having moved house and town, perhaps the rest of the family felt a separation with losing their father and like this wouldn't happen again with their youngest brother. There are no records of comments from the brothers or the community being concerned that Marvin would go the same way as his father, but sure enough, nine months after his father had died, Marvin Ronald Gibbs died on the 29th August 1966. Marvin too was determined to have an undiagnosed liver disease just like his father had, and Janie once again refused to have an autopsy performed. Perhaps Janie felt that performing an autopsy was an ungodly act that would in some way affect the chances of her family members getting into heaven? While the largest reason was most certainly to protect her own interests and for her to be able to complete her task, autopsy is a process rejected by many faiths and traditions. The police and staff at the insurance company pushed for autopsies as they felt that two deaths of this nature so close together and in one family didn't make sense. At this time, some members of the church community began to have suspicions about the deaths in the Gibbs family, but nobody wanted to be the one to come forward and accuse the pious and highly involved church member that Janie was. For many, there was still a huge disconnect. So even though the insurance company and the police of Crisp County were pressing for an autopsy on the body of young Marvin, Janie still had the support of the community enough to request that this procedure not be undertaken. Despite their suspicions, many in the community still felt that Janie wouldn't be capable of doing such a thing, particularly when it was to her own family that she seemed to have such an active devotion to.

Once again the church community poured support for the Gibb's family, offering counsel and companionship for Janie and her two remaining boys. When Marvin's life insurance came through, Janie once again provided a large portion of this claim to the church, which was undergoing significant renovations. While some began to talk about Janie seeming to almost be enjoying her new lifestyle, never being seen in the same dress and buying a new car, they could not help notice how generous she was also being with these funds. Those members of the community who still had faith in Janie chalked this spending down to a way to cope with her losses. However, Ellen Penny remained highly suspicious of Janie Gibbs. She didn't know how to speak out about her, both because she needed to live with the family and because she was so young, but after Marvin's death Ellen was certain that what was happening to the Gibbs family was no random or hereditary tragedy. Then, Melvin also began to fall ill.

As Melvin (often referred to in some articles as Lester) began to follow the path of his father and younger brother, the sixteen year old started to experience dizzy spells. Some people in the community attributed these headaches to puberty as the boy was sixteen. By this point, with such serious difficulties in the family, it is a wonder that Melvin's complaints weren't taken more seriously. He went downhill sharply. The doctors, not wanting to claim his death as another bout of undiagnosed liver disease that they weren't certain of, labeled his death a result of hepatitis. Once again a claim was made for life insurance, a portion donated to the church, and support lavished upon the Gibbs' family. At this point, Ellen became terrified for the life of her husband, herself, and their unborn child.

About a month after Melvin's death, Ellen and Roger's baby, Raymond, was born. Everybody noticed that Janie's mood lifted, and the community felt that this is where the horror ended for the Gibb's family. Janie was thrilled with her grandson, even though she had been so early married herself and her son had had his first child so early, making Janie a grandmother at thirty-four. Janie often used to show the baby to anybody who came around to the house, and would often be seen out with Raymond around the city. Ellen began to feel at ease around this time as Janie seemed to have changed entirely. The way that she interacted with Ellen seemed to have improved, and it seemed that the way that Janie went about all of her daily tasks with a different air.

However, even the baby began to fall ill soon. Ellen was in a state of desperation and didn't know what to do, the child only being one month old. The young girl has nobody that she could turn to, and didn't feel confident enough to make an accusation against Janie, even to her own husband. Despite the fact that Raymond was perfectly healthy, he died of an apparent heart condition. Everybody who was close to the Gibbs were completely shocked to hear of Raymond's death, and this is the point that many members of the congregation became highly suspicious of Janie. However, nobody did anything to prevent her from claiming the fifth and final member of her immediate family, her eldest and grieving son, with both Roger and Ellen still living with her at the time.

In the weeks after their baby died, Roger began to fall ill. Ellen, who was still under twenty at this age, had still not found the courage or the means to speak out against Janie. This may have been due to her living situation, or perhaps due to the sudden death of her son, but as Roger grew increasingly ill Ellen could do nothing but watch him deteriorate. She notes that during this time her husband constantly had red eyes, had visible rings around these, and was always pale and lacking in energy. He also used to get very severe headaches, but wasn't the type of person that liked to talk about any suffering that he was experiencing. The most that he would discuss these headaches was when he would be in such pain that he would be flinching. Ellen would ask if his head was giving him trouble again, to which he would respond with short and basic answers. Roger eventually found himself bedridden, being cared for by his mother. Despite what had happened to his father, two brothers, and own son, Roger never shared any suspicions about his mother with Ellen. It is entirely possible that he had figured out what was going on, being the last left, but didn't know how to get himself out of the situation.

Over the weeks, Roger's health got worse and worse. Ellen remembers overhearing an argument between Roger and his mother where he was repeatedly saying

"You did it! You did this to me!"

He was saying it over and over again as fiercely as he was able to in his deteriorated state. Ellen did not fully understand the conversation as she made sure that she kept out of sight. She asked Roger about it later in private, but he didn't reveal anything further and simply said that he and his mother had been squabbling over something. Ellen began to wonder whether she was paranoid about the situation, but it seemed that everything was pointing towards Janie's involvement in not only Roger's sickness but the suspicious deaths of the other four. Ellen stayed by her husband and cared for him as best she could, watching on as Janie nursed her son.

When Roger was eventually placed in hospital, Janie and Ellen spent nearly all of their time there. After a couple of days, Ellen noticed that Janie was in the habit of taking the water jug that the hospital placed in their room, tipping it down the sink, and replacing it with her own water. When Ellen asked her why she was doing this, Janie claimed that the hospital water had too much sulfur and that it hurt his throat. It was later realized that she was feeding her last remaining immediate family member increasing doses of arsenic through the water. Janie forced Roger to drink the water in large gulps and often. Once again, it is difficult to understand why this behavior was accepted by nurses, and also why nobody gave Roger testing for arsenic poisoning when four members of his family had died so suspiciously. However, even though this was a fairly common way for women to kill at the time, it is not until later years that we realized the signs and hints that might have saved the Gibbs family from their wife and mother.

One day, Janie asked Ellen to give Roger some water. Janie filled up a tall glass and placed it in Ellen's hand. Ellen gave Roger a small sip, but Janie demanded that he finish the whole glass, telling her that his throat is dry and he needs more. Ellen tipped the whole glass of water down her husband's throat, unknowingly giving him the final and strongest dose of arsenic. Perhaps Janie had been hoping that the blame might be placed on Ellen, or maybe she got satisfaction out of Ellen being the one that finally killed Roger, Janie having never been too keen on the girl. As Janie didn't want an autopsy on Roger, just like it was for the others, it is hard to say whether this act was a final insurance in her mind of her not being guilty of the crime, or whether it was the latter and she got satisfaction out of Ellen killing her spouse unintentionally. It is also possible, with Roger being left for last, that she was the least willing to kill him and needed Ellen to perform this final duty. After all, it would have made sense to kill the older two sons first and leave the younger one in her care, Marvin being so young and the least able of all three brothers to be able to take any action against his mother even if he had figured out what was happening. This suggests that Roger might have been somewhat of a favorite of Janie's, and that she wanted as much time with him as she could. Whatever the reason, Roger died soon after receiving the dose. He was only nineteen, and this finished Janie's work, whether it was insurance fraud or what she perceived to be God's work.

Just as she had with her two younger sons and her husband, Janie attempted to stop medical professionals from undertaking autopsies on Roger and Raymond Gibbs. However, as Ellen was the wife and mother, she has the rights of next of kin. Autopsies were performed that revealed extremely high levels of arsenic in Roger's organs, around twenty times that which you would expect to find in a body during an autopsy where arsenic has not been the cause of death. It was at this time that the Crisp County police called for the bodies of Charles, Marvin, and Melvin to be exhumed. People crowded around at the graveyard to watch while the bodies were taken out of the ground and placed on blue tarps. People began to say that they had thought there was something suspicious the whole time. A lot of guilt began to spread through the community. What if they had mentioned something earlier? Would they have at least been able to save the lives of Roger and his infant son? Mothers who had given their children to Janie to look after day in and day out felt embarrassed about their judgment of her character. This time the sympathy poured out for young Ellen who has lost her home, husband, and baby all within the space of a month. All five murders were committed in a short period of time, between 1966 and 1967. In all, Janie had received $31 000 in life insurance payments and given around ten percent of this to the church, but now she would have to answer for the crimes that she had done against those in the world that trusted her the most. Eric Hickey who has performed a study on female serial killers including Janie Lou Gibbs in 1991 claims that "These are the *quiet killers*, every bit as lethal as male serial murderers, but we are seldom aware of one in our midst because of their low visibility." Hickey also found that it takes an average of eight years to catch a female serial killer, nearly double what it takes on average to identify and arrest male serial killers.

Janie was arrested on Christmas Eve 1967, the day before her thirty-fifth birthday. She admitted to having killed all five of her immediate family members, but claimed that she didn't have a motive for doing so. While many people claim that she did this for the insurance money, there is still the chance that she genuinely committed the crimes in the name of her fanatic religious beliefs, wanting her family to be with her in heaven.

By February, Janie was determined to be insane and not fit for a trial but it was still agreed that she should not be able to live out her life in the community as she had been before. Janie took up residence at a state mental hospital where she served as a hospital cook, living there until 1976. At this time, multiple people had testified that they thought Janie was aware enough of her actions that she should have to deal with their legal ramifications. On May 9th 1976, Janie was convicted for her crimes and handed down five life sentences, one for each family member that she had poisoned. Janie's sister came to visit her in an attempt to understand the things that Janie has done, but found that she was largely nonresponsive and bewildered. The first question that her sister asked was *Why did you kill your family, Janie?* To which Janie responded she didn't know. Her sister attempted again, saying *Do you feel guilty?* Janice once again responded that she didn't know, seeming to be removed and numbed to the situation. Her sister made one final attempt to reach out to Janie and understand what had happened, asking *Can I do anything to help you?* For the third time, Janie responded that she didn't know. Her sister continued to visit her in jail in an attempt to understand more about Janie, what she had done, and what she was going through. But it seemed that no matter how much she tried, Janie was like a shell of what she had previously been.

She came up for parole seventeen times but was denied on each occasion. In April of 1999, due to her failing health as a result of Parkinson's disease, Janie was released into her sister's care. The last years of her life were spent in a wheel chair at a nursing home in Douglasville, Georgia, where she died on February 7th 2010. She now rests in the Sunrise Memorial Gardens at Lithia Springs in Douglas County, Georgia.

BLACK WIDOW JUDY BUENOANO

ERIN CARTER

Judy Buenoano loved men. But she loved killing them more.

In 1971, she murdered her husband James and nine years later she would kill her own son, Michael. In 1983, she would attempt but fail to kill her boyfriend, John Gentry. She is also believed to have been responsible for the death of Bobby Joe Morris (another boyfriend) in 1978. She was never convicted of the Morris crime, however, as by the time the authorities had connected the dots she was sentenced to death for the murder of her first husband.

But the suspicions didn't stop with the Morris death. Buenoano is also suspected of killing a man in 1974 and in 1980, another boyfriend would die under suspicious circumstances.

Buenoano would become the first woman executed in Florida since 1848 and only the third woman executed since capital punishment had been reinstated in 1976.

She would be sent to the electric chair in 1998. Her last words were that she wanted to be remembered as a "good mother."

Instead, she would go down as one of the most sadistic female serial killers in American history.

This is her story.

EARLY LIFE

Judy was born Judias Welty in Quanah, Texas on April 4th, 1943. Her father was a day laborer at a local farm. Judy would talk about her mother being a full-blooded member of the Mesquite Apache tribe but little did she know that a "Mesquite Apache" tribe didn't exist.

Her mother would die of tuberculosis when Judy was only two years old. She and her baby brother Robert would be sent to live with their grandparents while their two older siblings would be put up for adoption.

"When Judy's mother died," forensic psychologist Paula Orange said. "It sent Judy's life into a tailspin. This is one of those 'Butterfly Effect' scenarios. A tragic circumstance that occurred early in a child's life that led to her perpetuating pain on everyone else for the rest of her own adult life."

She would eventually leave her grandparents and join her father in Roswell, New Mexico. He had remarried and Judy would claim that both he and her new stepmother would beat, starve, and burn her with cigarettes.

They made her a "house slave", forcing her to do chores around the house at their bidding. Judy would finally act out at the age of fourteen as she would burn two of her step brothers with hot grease. Not stopping there, she attacked both her father and step-mom with fists flying.

Police would be called and Judy would be jailed for over two months. After she served her jail time, the judge gave Judy a choice, either return home or go to reform school. She opted for the latter and was sent to Foothills High School. She would remain there until 1959 when she would graduate at the age of sixteen.

She held her entire family in contempt, particularly her younger brother Robert.

"I wouldn't spit down his throat if his guts were on fire," Judy once said when asked about her brother.

CHANGING IDENTITY

Judy returned to Roswell but changed her name to "Anna Schultz". She found work as a nurse aide and would give birth to a baby boy out of wedlock, Michael Schultz on March 30, 1961. Judy would remain silent on the identity of the baby's father but people believed that Judy was having an affair with a pilot from the nearby air force base.

In 1963, the twenty-two-year-old Judy would marry James Goodyear. Goodyear was twenty-nine years old and serving as a sergeant in the United States Air Force.

They would have their first child together, James Jr, four years later. James would celebrate the event by legally adopting Michael. Daughter Kimberly would come a year later as the family would move to Orlando, Florida.

Judy would then open her own business, starting the Conway Acres Child Care Center in Orlando. She listed James as the co-owner even though he was during a one-year tour in the Vietnam War. After returning home, he only had three months of downtime before he was admitted to the U.S. Naval Hospital in Orlando, complaining from symptoms staff physicians never quite identified. He would die on September 15, 1971.

Goodyear was only thirty-seven years old at the time of death and authorities believed he died due to natural causes.

"He came home from Vietnam ill and he never got well," Judy said. "It had nothing to do with me. I was not in Vietnam."

"Crazy that Goodyear was able to survive the horrors of Vietnam but not Judy Buenoano," Orange said. "He had no idea he was married to a sociopath. She had no respect for the fact that he had just put himself on the line for her and the country. All she saw were dollar signs."

Judy poisoned James with arsenic and waited almost a week after his death before cashing in his three life insurance policies. A few months later, an "accidental fire" burned down their Orlando home. Judy would receive another $90,000 in fire insurance.

She lost her husband and her home. But her purse was never fatter.

NO GRIEVING WIDOWS ALLOWED

Judy would waste no time finding another man. Despite having three kids in tow, she would find a new love in Bobby Joe Morris when she moved her family to Pensacola.

It was business as usual for Judy as she had a fat bank account courtesy of James Goodyear and a new beau in Bobby Joe. Eldest son Michael, however, was not doing well in school. He scored on the low end on IQ tests and was a behavioral problem. Judy would get him evaluated at a state hospital in 1974 and then sent Michael out to foster care where he would also receive psychiatric treatment.

Judy's new home would suffer another "accidental fire" and she collected money from the insurance. She then took Michael out of foster care and moved to Trinidad, Colorado with Bobby Joe and the rest of her children. Judy then changed her name from "Anna Schultz" to "Judias Morris".

FOUR YEARS MAX

Judy would date Bobby Joe for four years before deciding it was time to cut him loose.

Bobby Joe would start to suffer from the same mysterious illness as James Goodyear did years earlier as he complained of dizziness and vomiting. He would be admitted to San Rafael Hospital on January 4, 1978, but doctors would not be able to pinpoint what was wrong with him. He would be sent home to Judy's care two weeks later. Two days later, however, he would would pitch face-first into his dinner plate, unconscious. He would be rushed to the hospital, but Judy knew that her "medicine" had taken effect.

Five days later, Bobby Joe Morris would be dead. Doctors would chalk up his death to cardiac arrest and metabolic acidosis.

Judy would wait, just like she did after she killed James, before cashing in on Bobby Joe's life insurance.

Authorities were none the wiser.

But Bobby Joe's family suspected something fishy was going on. Back in 1974, Judy and Bobby Joe had been visiting Brewton, Alabama when a man from Florida was found dead in a motel room in that town. Police would find the man in the room after receiving an anonymous call. He was shot in the chest with a .22-caliber weapon and his throat was cut open.

Judy's connection to the crime? Bobby Joe's mother had overheard Judy telling her son about the murder.

"The sonofabitch shouldn't have come up here in the first place," Judy said. "If he came up here he was gonna die."

Bobby Joe had told his mother about the crime on his deathbed. She thought the confession could be attributed to his delirium, but Bobby Joe told her too many specifics to ignore.

"We should never had done that terrible thing," Bobby Joe mumbled to his mother. "Never should have done that to him."

She tipped off police but they would not be able to find any fingerprints inside the room and no bullet was recovered from the corpse. The case remained unsolved.

WHAT'S ONE MORE SURNAME?

On May 3rd, 1978, Judy would change her name again. This go around, she would change her last name to Buenoano, which in Spanish meant "good year." She stated that she meant it as a tribute to her husband James Goodyear and her Apache mother.

Things continued to go bad with Michael as he dropped out of high school in the tenth grade. With limited employment opportunities, he would join the army in June of 1979 and get assigned to Ft. Benning in Georgia after basic training. When he was on his way to his new post, he visited Judy in Pensacola.

Judy greeted her son with open arms. Then she began poisoning him.

By the time he reached Ft. Benning, he felt sick. Army physicians would find seven times the normal level of arsenic in his body.

They could do little to reverse the damage done. Six weeks after his arrival, the muscles in his arms and legs and deteriorated to the point where he was a paraplegic.

"Michael had no use of his legs," Orange said. "And he could not move his arms past his elbow. Again, Judy was a sociopath. It is unfathomable for a normal human being, a mother, to do this to her own child. Yet she did it to Michael. He was always an inconvenience to her but now that he had military insurance he could become an asset in death."

Judy would give Michael the short shrift while favoring James and Kimberly. Michael and James didn't get along well as clearly their mother favored the latter. Judy would hide Michael when people came over because she was ashamed of him. She would have a neighbor named Constance Lang watch over him when visitors arrived.

"Michael didn't fit the picture Judy wanted to present to the world," Orange said. "She wanted to be looked at like a woman of high status. She drove a Corvette and owned her own business. Michael was a slow-thinking kid. She didn't want anyone to see that."

The army didn't investigate the reasons behind Michael's inordinate levels of arsenic. Instead, they set him up with leg braces and a prosthetic device on one of his arms.

He would be discharged from active duty because of the medical disability.

But his mother saw dollar signs.

The day after his return home, Judy wasted no time. She organized a fishing trip with Michael, James, and daughter Kimberly. They would leave Kimberly ashore at the East River bridge while they went into the water with a two-seat canoe. A small folding lawn chair had been placed in the middle of the canoe for Michael who had was outfitted with a leg brace, a fishing reel, and a ski belt.

James would state that had fished for about two hours when they were reaching shore when a "snake fell into the canoe." He said that everyone panicked as the snake slithered around. The canoe hit a log and capsized.

James would claim to have been knocked out by the impact and would remember nothing until he came to inside an ambulance.

He would tell this version to the court but when he was talking to Army investigators, he made no mention of a snake.

"There is conjecture as to how much James was involved or much did he know," Orange said. "The statement given to the army investigators is different from what he would state later in court. The statement given to the army was a written statement and the handwriting didn't seem to match his own."

A man named Ricky Hicks saw the overturned canoe, an ice chest, and a plastic bag in the river. He also saw Judy and James.

"I lost the other boy," Judy said as Ricky approached them on the shore. "A snake had gotten into the canoe and I tried to hold the snake down with a paddle."

"Where is he?"

"It's no use," Judy said, waving him off.

Hicks said Judy appeared to be concerned about James then asked him for a beer. He then drove Judy's car to a nearby phone and called the county rescue squad.

The rescue team arrived and began looking for the missing Michael.

The canoe had not moved as there was barely a current. They would find Michael's body one-quarter of a mile upriver where the canoe had been rescued. The rescuers stated that it should not have been a problem to swim upstream, suggesting that Michael could have been saved.

Judy initially said that Michael had a life jacket on but later recanted and said that it was a ski belt.

There was no ski belt on Michael when he was found.

Judy would later state that after the canoe capsized, she saw James lying face down in the water. She swam over and cleared his air passage to resuscitate him. She looked around for Michael then was picked up by Ricky Hicks.

"Michael disappeared under water," Judy said. "I went to rescue James. I almost lost both of my sons that day. Mothers just don't murder their children. If I'd have lost both of them, I don't know what I would have done. They would have had to put me in a mental institution."

"Kimberly's boyfriend would later testify that Judy had killed Michael for the insurance money," Orange said. "The children knew about their mother but she had clearly brainwashed them into silence. She provided for them, she fed them. She knew what was best."

Telling the police that she was a "clinical physician", they bought her story of the boat capsizing. The army investigators did not buy her account. Not having any evidence, however, they would eventually pay her Michael's military life insurance ($20,000). Investigators got suspicious, however, when they found out that two civilian life policies were taken out on Michael. The applications on both policies look to have been forged.

Judy's former sister-in-law, Peggy Goeller, would call to inquire how she was doing. She would make no mention of Michael's death during her first call but on a second call she told Peggy that Michael had died "during Army maneuvers".

MOVING ON

Judy would demonstrate very little grief over Michael's death and she would not be charged with his murder. Foremost on her mind was finding another man and another big check.

She opened a beauty salon in Gulf Breeze and found her next mark: businessman John Gentry.

Gentry was more well-heeled than her previous conquests so Judy put on airs for his sake. She told him that she had Ph.D.'s in biochemistry and psychology and was the former head of nursing at West Florida Hospital.

Gentry believed her story and decided to spoil his blue-blooded girlfriend expensive gifts, vacations and the finest cuisine all in the name of courtship.

Pushing the envelope, Judy would encourage John to provide life insurance for both them both. She then secretly boosted Gentry's coverage from $50,000 to $500,000 without him knowing.

Two months later, Judy began giving Gentry "vitamin pills".

"Come on," she said, placing two pills into Gentry's palm.

"What are you, my mother?" Gentry asked.

"Well, God forbid I want to see you healthy," Judy slid the cup of water toward her prey.

Gentry would then complain of dizziness and later begin vomiting after his daily dose of Judy's "vitamins."

He would admit himself into the hospital and noticed that his symptoms disappeared when he stopped taking the vitamins.

Still smitten by Judy, he did not suspect her of wrongdoing. Instead, he took her vitamins and hid them in his briefcase.

One night, however, Judy sat him down for a special dinner. She had a very special announcement.

"I'm pregnant," she said, smiling in triumph.

"Finally," Gentry said. He told Judy that they should celebrate. She told him to go to the liquor store for an expensive bottle of champagne.

"Be right back," he said, kissing her with excitement.

Running out the door, Gentry got into his car and a bomb exploded with he turned the ignition key.

Amazingly, Gentry survived the blast as trauma surgeons saved his life.

"Judy really overplayed her hand with the explosion in the car," Orange said. "Really it speaks to her level of dedication and ingenuity. Who knows where she got the idea, maybe watching the Godfather. But the police found the dynamite residue inside Gentry's car. They decided to look no further than to Judy herself."

Their interrogation and research would unearth lie after lie. They found out about the $450,000 increase in Gentry's life insurance.

Gentry himself thought the insurance had been canceled. He was shocked to learn that she had increased the payout and was paying his premiums out of her own pocket. The police didn't spare him any quarter. They would him that she was not a real doctor and that she couldn't get pregnant.

"What?" Gentry muttered, completely flabbergasted.

Judy had been sterilized seven years earlier.

Gentry couldn't believe his ears. Police would go on to say that she had booked tickets for a world cruise for herself and her children...leaving Gentry out. They discovered that Judy had been telling her friends that Gentry was suffering from a "terminal illness."

The only "terminal illness" Gentry had was Judy Buenoano.

Now fully convinced, Gentry would reach into his briefcase and give police the "vitamin pills" that Judy had been giving him.

"Judy was emptying the vitamin casing and filling it with formaldehyde and a little arsenic," Orange said. "Over time, this would have been lethal."

The state attorney would refuse to charge Judy as they wanted an air tight case in order to prosecute. Knowing that they had their killer, officers, and federal agents searched Judy's home in Gulf Breeze, obtaining wire and tape from her bedroom that looked to match the same wire/tape they found on the bomb in Gentry's car.

They would search her son James' room, finding marijuana and a sawed-off shotgun. He would be jailed him for possession of drugs and an illegal weapon.

"Again, this is a strange mistake on Judy's part," Orange said. "She was meticulous and a good liar. Why she didn't remove any and all evidence from her home is a head-scratcher. She had gotten sloppy because she had gotten away with so many crimes before without so much as a slap on the wrist. She thought she was above the law, got careless and left incriminating evidence behind."

Judy would then be arrested at her beauty salon and charged with attempted murder. It took a month of police work, but authorities would trace the source of the dynamite used in the bomb, linking the Alabama buyer to Judy via phone records which showed numerous long-distance calls from her home.

Judy would pay bail but authorities would not let up. Five months later, she would be indicted for first-degree murder in the death of her son Michael, with an additional count of grand theft for the insurance scam.

Feeling the noose around her neck, Judy would fake a seizure and wind up in Santa Rosa Hospital.

Authorities then exhumed the bodies of the men they believed she killed. Bobby Joe Morris was exhumed with arsenic found in his remains. Identical results were obtained with the exhumation of James Goodyear, in the following month.

Connecting the dots, police obtained a court order to exhume the bodies of all the men that had died while associated with Judy; son Michael, husband James Goodyear, and boyfriend Bobby Joe Morris.

Arsenic would be found in all of the bodies.

"There was enough arsenic in him (Goodyear) to kill twelve people," Detective Ted Chamberlain said. "So he was loaded. I mean that boy was loaded with it when he went down."

OPEN AND SHUT CASE

In 1984, Judy would be convicted of the murders of Michael and attempted murder of Gentry. In a separate trial in 1985, she would be convicted of the murder of James Goodyear in which she would ultimately receive the death sentence.

Judy would be imprisoned in the Florida Department of Corrections Broward Correctional Institution death row for women.

HER FINAL HOURS

Judy would spend her last day watching a hunting and fishing show, eating chocolates, and talking about old times with her children and cousin Jeanne Eaton. She would read a suspense novel called "Remember Me" and her last meal with be steamed broccoli, asparagus, strawberries and hot tea.

Judy's impending execution did not receive the same media attention as Karla Faye Tucker whose was executed only a month earlier. Her execution was opposed by the Pope and Jesse Jackson.

"'She may not have been as photogenic, as young or as pretty as Karla, but she was just as good a Christian," Eaton said.

"Judy obviously had her enablers within her family," Orange said. "How could she be 'just as good a Christian' if she is poisoning people, blowing them up and the 'Christian' she is being compared to is ice-picking people to death. People say the strangest things."

But Judy herself was bitter that no one paid much attention to her presence on death row, particularly the fact that she was a woman.

``Karla was a young female, very attractive and she had become a Christian in prison," Judy said. ``We all prayed that she would be granted a stay of execution and clemency because we felt that she was a different person and she deserved a chance. Possibly, I am a different person. But I was a Christian when I came here. I was a devout Catholic. I've not changed in that."

"It was a bit of a curiosity as to why the media was so charged to prevent the execution of Karla Faye Tucker and paid little heed to Buenoano," Orange said. "Tucker's killings were ferocious and sadistic while Buenoano's killings could be seen as passive. But what drew people to Tucker was her physical appearance and demeanor. She came across as a sweet, reformed choir girl at the end. She had a charming smile and a soft voice. Buenoano, on the other hand, looked sinister. She had squinty eyes, high cheekbones and a snarling, Southern drawl. Her body language and demeanor screamed hostile."

Judy would enter the death chamber with several guards by her side. They strapped her into the large oak chair, placing leather straps over her waist, wrists, chest, and legs.

They fitted the calf and headpiece electrodes last, inserting a wet sponge in between to reduce the burning of Judy's skin.

"Do you have a final statement?" the warden asked.

"No, sir," Judy closed her eyes tight.

The witnesses on the other side of the glass partition watched in silence.

Judy did not look at them as a leather mask was placed over her face.

The warden nodded his head and the switch was pulled.

Steam wafted up from her right leg as her body jolted for thirty-eight seconds. Her hands balled into fists, white knuckling from the shock as smoke rose from her feet to the ceiling.

Then Judy went limp. She would be pronounced dead at 7:08 a.m., March 30th, 1998.

The date was her son Michael's 37th birthday.

BLACK WIDOW KRISTIN ROSSUM
AIMEE BAXTER

Photos of a beautiful, lively little girl, her blonde hair in pigtails as she dances The Nutcracker in her little pink tutu. That same adorable child laughingly enjoying holidays with her family at their home. These are the pictures that Constance Rossum will show you of her daughter Kristin.

Bright, vivacious, and uncommonly beautiful are the words used to describe Kristin Rossum as a child. The child that everyone said was so smart and pretty, the one who modeled for department stores and who excelled in her schoolwork, the one with what seemed to be the perfect suburban childhood.

However, as many already know ... looks can be deceiving.

Idyllic Child becomes a Rebellious Teen

Born to Ralph and Constance Rossum on October 25, 1976, in Claremont, California, Kristin Rossum wanted for nothing. Kristin was the first child of Ralph Rossum – a professor at Claremont McKenna College – and his wife Constance – who worked at Azusa Pacific University. Even when her first and then second little brother was born, Kristin remained her parent's sweet little princess.

When Ralph accepted a position as President of Hampden-Sydney College in southern Virginia, the family moved across the country from California to Virginia. It was 1991 and Kristin was a delicate 15 years old. Her parents enrolled her in an all-girl boarding school in Richmond, Virginia named St. Catherine's School.

That seems to be the beginning of the end of Kristin's innocence. At the private school, Kristin made friends quickly and soon was very popular. She became the party girl smoking, drinking, and using marijuana liberally.

In 1992, at just 16 years old, Kristin is introduced to methamphetamines – a strong Central Nervous System (CNS) stimulant – and is soon hooked. Within a few weeks, she was using Crystal Meth (also known as Crank, Speed, Chalk, etc.) daily. She was a tweaker (slang used to describe a methamphetamine addict).

Kristin the Druggie

When asked about it later, Kristin recalled her first time using meth by saying "I remember it feeling good, a kind of euphoria. You feel very revved up and energetic and happy. I wanted to feel that all the time."

Soon, Kristin's straight As were slipping to become Cs and Ds. She lost weight rapidly and began to withdraw from her family and any friends who were not using meth. According to later court records, Kristin is described as having "an almost insatiable need for crystal meth."

It was not long before Kristin developed all the character traits that addicts hone to conceal and continue their freedom to use. Lying, manipulation, and theft became the new norm for young Kristin Rossum.

Her parents were understandably at a loss for how to deal with this behavior. After all, not that long ago they were tucking her into her pink canopy bed and kissing her goodnight with a song and a prayer. However, the lack of consequences established by her parents could be a contributing factor in her later misdeeds.

At first, they ignored their daughter's erratic and rapidly devolving character, chalking it up to teenage angst. Eventually, they could not turn a blind eye anymore and they soon realized that their daughter was not who they thought she was.

Later, both Ralph and Constance cite an incident in 1993 as the first time they admitted their daughter had a problem. After returning from a cruise in April of that year, the Rossums found that their sweet, perfect daughter had in fact stolen their credit cards, personal checks, and a video camera.

Confronted with the missing items, Kristin pointed to some of her friends (fellow druggies) as the thieves. They say that she admitted to using some of the cash to buy drugs but insisted that the rest was stolen by somebody else. Her parents accepted Kristin's excuse and did not report the theft to police.

According to Constance's testimony later, Kristin's erratic behavior came to a head in December of 1993. Ralph Rossum – convinced Kristin was still using drugs – attempted to search his daughter's backpack. She resisted, they struggled, and he struck her several times in the arm to get the bag away from her.

However, that was not the end of the incident. Sobbing and enraged, Kristin grabbed a knife from the kitchen and slashed at her wrists. When that did not work, she ran upstairs to the bathroom, locked herself inside, and began hacking at her wrists with a razor. Later Kristin told the court, "I felt devastated ... I didn't know how to deal with the situation ... I wanted them to see how sorry I was."

Her wounds, however, were superficial and her parents treated them at home. They later said that they were "afraid of what would happen if they took her to the hospital." They feared that if they told the hospital that she had cut herself, they would have committed her for a psychiatric evaluation and if they tested her blood and found drugs, they would report her to the police.

It is likely that the reason none of the cuts were serious was that Kristin did not intend them to be. Psychologists later speculated that it was merely a way for her to manipulate her parents. If it was, it worked.

Again, Kristin escaped any immediate consequences for her bad behavior. Again, her parents made excuses for her behavior and thus enable her to continue that behavior. Cryptically, one entry in her diary after this incident contained the morbidly, prophetic words, "I could get away with murder."

A few days after this incident, a teacher noticed the marks on Kristin (or she possibly showed them to her intentionally). She called the police to the school to investigate the possibility of child abuse.

Officer Larry Horowitz of the Claremont Police investigated and testified that Kristin told him that her father had hit her and that her mother had "called her a slut and said she was worthless." After interviewing Ralph and Constance Rossum, Officer Horowitz concluded that there had been no abuse and the case was closed.

In January 1994, Constance found a glass pipe hidden in Kristin's underwear drawer. She eventually called Officer Horowitz and Kristin was handcuffed, arrested, and held for several hours at Claremont Municipal Jail.

Kristin finally had her first taste of culpability. She seemed to clean her act up and after graduating, she enrolled part-time at the University of Redlands in California. However, soon she relapsed and dropped out of school without a word to her family and simply disappeared. She moved to Chula Vista – a suburb of San Diego near the Mexican border.

A Chance Encounter

After a month of hard partying, drinking, smoking meth, and hiding from her parents, Kristin was walking the pedestrian bridge that led from Chula Vista to Tijuana, Mexico. Authorities speculate that at the time she was likely on her way to meet her supplier in Mexico on that fateful day.

As she crossed the bridge, Kristin Rossum dropped her jacket. Before she could retrieve it, a handsome young man that she later described as reminding her of John Stamos, had picked it up and was handing it to her. It was Greg de Villers and he later told friends "it was love at first sight." They chatted in French while Greg's younger brother paced nearby.

She returned to the Southern California apartment where de Villers lived with his brothers, Bertrand and Jerome, and a friend, Christopher Wren. She never left.

Within a few weeks, the couple was professing their love and de Villers had sworn to help Kristin kick her meth addiction. Greg's brothers and Wren were not happy and prompted him to end the relationship. They had noticed that things were coming up missing from the apartment since Kristin's arrival and knew of her drug problem.

According to a statement given later by de Villers' friend and roommate Christopher Wren, Kristin had told him that she felt like being with Greg was the wrong choice. For some reason, Wren chose not to tell his buddy.

Even if Wren had told de Villers about Kristin's doubts, it is unlikely that it would have made any difference. Greg de Villers was adamant, he loved Kristin Rossum no matter what her faults and he was going to save her from herself.

By May of 1995, it looked as though he had done just that. By all accounts, it looked like Kristin was clean and free of the hold meth had on her. She reestablished contact with her worried parents and it looked like Kristin was finally moving towards the bright future her parents had envisioned for their little girl.

The Rossums looked at Greg de Villers as if he was an angel for all that he had done for Kristin. Constance Rossum, in an interview with the CBS news magazine "48 Hours," put it like this, "We always called Greg our godsend from heaven. I mean, of all the people she could have met, to have met a nice, decent person who wanted to take care of her, we thanked God."

Soon, Kristin enrolled at San Diego State University. Her professors later said described Rossum as a stellar student with one going so far as to describe her as "among the most promising students" he had "ever taught."

Everyone who knew her believed she was happy. She was earning straight As and in 1998, she graduated cum laude (with honors). She got a job at San Diego Medical Examiner's office as a toxicologist.

Constance would later testify, "Our old Kristin was back," and she thanked God and de Villers – in that order – for the change.

Storybook Love?

Everyone who knew them described Kristin and Greg as the perfect couple. Constance Rossum testified later that when they were together they were "like a couple of lovebirds." When they announced their engagement, nobody was surprised.

However, as is often the case, outward appearances did not accurately represent reality. There was a layer of tension beneath the surface of de Villers and Rossum's storybook love affair. Kristin's closest friends knew that she had a hard time staying faithful and monogamous.

According to prosecutor's later, Kristin actually maintained a "graphically flirtatious" correspondence with a former boyfriend and at least one other man during at least some portion of her relationship with de Villers. Rossum even went to her mother only a month before she was supposed to walk down the aisle and broke down in tears as she told her mother that she wanted to cancel the wedding.

Constance Rossum considered her daughter's outburst to be cold feet, pre-wedding jitters that would pass. After all, Greg de Villers was the man who led her out of the darkness of addiction and Constance could not see how Kristin could possibly want to end the relationship.

She would soon tell the court, "I gave her the wrong counsel, I'm afraid."

The wedding was spectacular. The video shows a smiling and laughing Kristin Rossum, now Kristin de Villers, dancing with her new husband and looking happy. As for de Villers, he is recorded on that video saying, "Kristin is the most wonderful person I've ever met. I just can't wait to spend the rest of my life with her."

Only seven months after the wedding, however, Kristin Rossum told her mother that she felt "trapped like a bird in a cage." It was January 2000 and Kristin's journal shows that she had begun souring on her marriage only a couple of months after the wedding.

Greg de Villers did not show any sign that he felt the same or even knew of his wife's misgivings and doubt. Conversely, his brother Jerome later testified that Greg was ecstatically happy and never spoke of anything even smacking of marital discord. Even his colleagues at a genetics research firm where de Villers worked, described him as happily married and devoted to his wife. Some even went so far as to describe Greg de Villers as "sickeningly in love with his wife."

Friends of Greg de Villers said that he was often talking about his plans for their future together. He bragged about his wife's accomplishments, both big and small, and often spoke of starting a family. One friend remembers him saying that he wanted "all girls who were as beautiful and smart as Kristin."

At the same time, his adored wife was painting a much grimmer portrait of her marriage and her husband. She often complained to colleagues and friends about Greg, saying that he was moody, controlling, and domineering. Later, in an interview with "48 Hours," Kristin said, "Greg became very, very clinging... I tried to pull away and have some sort of independence."

An email sent to her brother Brent only 11 months after the wedding showed how she truly felt. She wrote, "I should have trusted my own instincts and called off the wedding. Now I'm stuck with the heavy realization that I married the wrong person."

A New Love Affair

Not long after Kristin Rossum sent that email to her brother, she met Dr. Michael Robertson. Newly hired as Chief Toxicologist at the San Diego Medical Examiner's office, Robertson was Kristin's immediate supervisor and she began spending large amounts of time with him.

Soon, they were spending time together outside of work. Kristin found danger and excitement in her passionate affair with her handsome, Australian doctor – who was also married. Her husband – and the problems she seemed to have with him – disappeared from Kristin's consideration and soon she was talking with friends outside of her colleagues about the wonderful new man in her life who she described as "a big hunk of an Australian guy."

By early May, Rossum was receiving inappropriate emails and notes from her boss. A search of her desk later turned up love notes and IOUs for things such as "a night of lovemaking" from Robertson. Coworkers later reported that Robertson was often seen sauntering into work with a bouquet of flowers that would soon end up on Rossum's desk.

In June, according to court records, Kristin Rossum had given her lover a gift. A book titled "52 Invitations To Great Sex" she had inscribed on the inside cover, "Well, sweetheart, together we'll enjoy a lifetime of passion."

When asked later, Rossum said, "I felt like I was in love. It was very romantic, very exciting, very passionate."

In August of 2000, Kristin turned to her best friend, Melissa Prager. Prager later told the court that he friend confided in her that she was madly in love with Robertson but was "terrified" by the idea of telling Greg she wanted a divorce.

In October 2000, Greg de Villers was still telling his friends, family, co-workers, and anyone else who would listen about his love for his wife and his plans for their future. His brother Jerome later told the court that around Halloween, Greg was talking about his excitement over taking his future children with Kristin out to trick or treat.

However, Kristin Rossum had reached a conclusion about her marriage. She told her close friends that she was looking for an apartment and planned to leave her husband.

'Til Death Do Us Part

It is unclear how de Villers learned of his wife's infidelity and plan to leave him. Rossum has always claimed that she told Greg de Villers about the affair and that her admission launched a spiraling depression in her husband.

According to Kristin Rossum, she told her husband about Robertson and he demanded the man's phone number. When Kristin supplied the number (although why she would is uncertain), de Villers called her boss and lover and demanded that he break off their relationship.

There is no court record of a response to this demand by Robertson. However, the relationship continued.

Authorities, however, have a very different set of circumstances in mind for how Greg discovered Kristin's infidelity.

They maintain that de Villers found out about the affair on accident in the fall of 2000. This was after Kristin and Robertson were sent to Milwaukee together to attend a toxicology conference. According to court records, despite being booked into separate hotels – likely due to rumors in the office about their relationship – the duo rented their own room together and spent several nights from September 30 to October 7 together in that room.

A coworker saw Kristin at the conference during the week and noted that she was no longer wearing her wedding ring.

One of the conferences that Rossum and Robertson attended in Milwaukee was on the deadly effects of fentanyl. Fentanyl is a clear, odorless narcotic that is 100 times stronger than morphine. It is generally administered to cancer patients whose pain is not eased by other means. It is so potent that it only takes a few drops to kill.

The seminar also discussed the fact that the drug is so rarely prescribed and used that most medical examiner's offices do not test for it. Both Rossum and Robertson were well aware of the fact that their office did not test for fentanyl.

During the three years that Rossum had worked in the San Diego Medical Examiner's office, only seven cases of death by overdose had involved fentanyl. She had seen 15 patches and 1 vial of the drug in a powder form. It was Rossum's job to log and track the drugs in her logbook. It was Robertson's job to hold the key to the cabinet those substances was then stored in.

These were facts that seemed innocuous at the time but would soon hold a more serious meaning.

Returning to Old Ways

Only a day or two after returning from Milwaukee, Rossum sent de Villers an email telling him that she was taking three different prescription drugs "to help with the severe anxiety I've been experiencing as a result of our relationship. You've hurt me beyond repair."

Not only was Kristin taking prescription medications, she had fallen back into her addiction to meth. After some of the drugs went missing from her office, Robertson admitted later that he found traces of the drug in her desk and rather than turning his girlfriend in, he flushed the drugs down the toilet. Then he covered for her with his superiors.

Once again, Kristin Rossum has done something bad. Once again, somebody shields her from the ramifications of her actions. Once again, there are no consequences for Kristin's bad actions.

Severing Ties

By early November 2000, Rossum was ready to end her relationship with de Villers. She insisted she wanted only a "trial separation."

She later told detectives that de Villers literally collapsed when she told him she was leaving him. She claimed that he lay in bed for days afterward and would not communicate with her. She later told the court, "It was painful for me, too, to see someone you love hurt so much." She still never owned up to the fact that it was her own actions that caused her husband that pain.

On November 6, 2000, just after 9:15 pm, Kristin Rossum called 991.

She claimed that her husband was unresponsive and that she was doing CPR to try and revive him. When paramedics arrived, however, they found Rossum on the phone in the living room. Her husband was lying lifeless on their bed.

Gregory de Villers lay dead in his La Jolla bedroom with rose petals covering his chest. Besides his lifeless head lay a copy of his wedding picture ... less than two years old. Nearby on the floor lay a crumpled love letter from the dashing Australian doctor that was his wife's boss and lover. Beside that was his wife's discarded diary, open to an entry that she had left confiding that she felt her marriage was the biggest mistake of her life.

For all intents and purposes, it looked like a suicide. His distraught widow claimed that Greg had learned that her affair with Robertson was still happening.

However, de Villers' brother Jerome adamantly refused to accept that his brother had committed suicide. The entire de Villers family demanded an investigation. Still, the San Diego police were hesitant to open an investigation.

The Truth and Nothing but the Truth

Their opinion quickly changed and authorities soon came to suspect Kristin Rossum, de Villers' 26-year-old blonde beauty of a wife. They believed that she had used her knowledge as a toxicologist and the information that she had gleaned from working in the medical examiner's office to poison her husband.

Due to concerns over a conflict of interest, de Villers' autopsy was outsourced to another lab in Los Angeles. That lab is one of the few in the country that tests for fentanyl. They found 7 times the lethal dose of fentanyl in de Villers' system.

Two weeks after de Villers' death, the San Diego police brought Kristin Rossum in for interrogation. She reiterated to police that her husband had been extremely depressed.

According to Kristin Rossum's story, on the Thursday before de Villers' death, they struggled over a letter that she had sticking out of her back pocket. In her account, de Villers' attempted to grab the letter from her pocket and knocked her to the ground to wrest it from her. She claimed that it was the first time she had been afraid of her husband.

When he had the letter, as Rossum's story goes, he held it out and threatened to take it to his wife's office and expose the affair as well as her reoccurring meth addiction. She took the letter and shredded it but de Villers pieced it back together.

In court, Rossum's parents described the night, two days before de Villers' death, when they went over to visit the couple for dinner. Ralph Rossum testified that de Villers seemed to be deeply depressed, "a man spiraling down."

Kristin Rossum's father continued to describe how de Villers had drunk heavily that night. He drank wine and gin until his father in law had to tell him to lower his voice. Constance Rossum described

Greg de Villers' voice as "fraught with melodrama" as he spoke at length about the dozen red roses that he had given to Kristin for her birthday a few days earlier.

She testified that he seemed depressed, agitated, and particularly obsessed with the fact that all but one had died and shed its petals. In a TV interview, she gave months after the death, Rossum stated, "He was making a big deal of the last rose standing. I think he was just making a statement that he knew our relationship was over."

Things rapidly spiraled from that point on. Police learned that Rossum had relapsed and was using meth again.

On June 25, 2001 – 7 months after Greg de Villers' death – his wife was arrested on charges of First Degree Murder. She spent over six months in jail and then on January 4, 2002, her parents posted $1.25 million for bail.

During the trial, the prosecution contended that she killed her husband to keep him from telling her bosses that she was having an affair with Robertson and that she was stealing meth from the office. They presented evidence that she had the knowledge about fentanyl to use it, access to the drug (remember the missing fentanyl from her office), and the motive to kill her husband.

On November 12, 2002, Kristin Rossum was found guilty of first-degree murder.

Exactly one month later on December 12, she was sentenced to life in prison without the chance of parole. She was transferred from the San Diego jail to the Central California Women's Facility in Chowchilla California – the largest women's correctional facility in the United States.

Distant Repercussions

In 2006, the de Villers family filed a lawsuit against Rossum and San Diego County for wrongful death. They were asking for $50 million but on March 25, 2006, a San Diego jury ordered Rossum to pay more than $100 million in punitive damages to the de Villers family. The same judge ordered San Diego County to pay $1.5 million.

According to the de Villers' lawyer John Gomez, the punitive damages awarded in this case are the most assessed against an individual defendant in California history. The jury apparently awarded double what the de Villers' family was asking for due to the estimation that Rossum could make $60 million from selling the rights to her story.

The judge later lowered the awarded amounts to $10 million in punitive damages and $4.5 million in a compensatory award.

In September of 2010, a 3-judge panel of the 9th US Circuit Court of Appeals ruled that Rossum's lawyers should have challenged the prosecutions assertion that she poisoned her husband with fentanyl by demanding their own tests. Due to this, the panel ordered a San Diego federal court to hold a hearing into whether the defense's error could have affected the trial's outcome.

On September 13, 2011, the US Court of Appeals withdrew its opinion and replaced it with a one-paragraph statement that denied Rossum's petition.

Conclusion

Kristin Rossum will spend the rest of her life behind bars. She has exhausted her state appeals and the federal courts denied her petition to be heard.

Her contention remains that her husband killed himself. She further believes that he did it the way that he did to point the finger of guilt at her. She vehemently insists that she did not kill her husband.

At one point, Kristin Rossum even suggested that her lover the handsome Australian doctor might have killed her husband. He knew about de Villers' threat to expose them before his death and had access to the fentanyl.

For his part, Robertson returned to Brisbane, Australia only one month after de Villers' death under the excuse that he had to care for his ailing mother. In September of 2013, the San Diego Reader reported that prosecutors filed a criminal complaint against Robertson in 2006 charging him with one count of conspiracy to obstruct justice.

If he returned to the US, Robertson could face up to three years in prison. In 2001, Robertson was named as an "unindicted co-conspirator" in Rossum's trial.

As of 2014, Robertson was running a forensic consulting business in Brisbane.

Kristin Rossum, the sweet spoiled only daughter of college professors, who was never held accountable for her actions as she grew up will spend the rest of her days within the walls of the largest women's correctional facility in the US. She is finally going to have to answer for what she has done.

BLACK WIDOW LYDA TRUEBLOOD

JESSI DILLARD

A true "black widow"

Death followed Lyda Trueblood everywhere she went. At first glance, it may have seemed that the young woman was facing a run of bad luck – but as the run continued, suspicions began to arise.

Northeast of Kansas City, in the small town of Keytesville, Missouri, a true "black widow" was born on October 16, 1892. Over the course of her life, Lyda Anna Mae Trueblood took on seven married names, and is most well-known as Lyda Southard. However, Idaho remembers her as Lady Bluebeard – the state's first female serial killer.

"She swept the men of her choice off their feet – courted them so persistently that they could not escape," said V. H. Ormsby, a deputy sheriff from Twin Falls, Idaho. Ormsby was one of the officers who arrested Trueblood in Honolulu for the death of her fourth husband.

By the age of 27, Trueblood had already killed six people, including her own daughter. However, she would only be convicted of one murder – the poisoning of her fourth husband, Edward Meyer, in 1921.

"The marital experiences of the one-time Missouri country town girl eclipses even those of fiction. Ten years ago, while still in her teens, she was attending Sunday school and enjoying the popularity that goes with being a village belle."

Described as "pudgy faced and plain of figure," Trueblood still caught the eye of Robert Dooley, whose family was close with Trueblood's. Some said Trueblood was the most popular girl at her high school, claiming she had an "indefinable something, a spark giving off a light that draws men, by physiological and chemical attraction."

"They wasn't so wealthy, just so-so," said Mrs. Larrabee Hanson, who lived near the Trueblood family. "But they were all church-going people, devout and clean-living. (Trueblood) went to church every Sunday without fail."

A magazine writer, Alan Jaffe, who detailed Trueblood's history for a profile in *Argosy* magazine in 1957, said men "hung around her like flies about a honey pot." In fact, when Trueblood finally left her childhood home and moved to Twin Falls, Robert Dooley followed – and the two were married there in 1912, when she was only 21.

A promise of the future

"They had a perfectly normal relationship," said Mychel Matthews with the Twin Falls County Historical Museum. "They appeared to be just like the rest of the residents around town."

With the security of their future family in mind, the newlyweds decided to take out an insurance policy on Robert and his brother, Edward. If either died, the survivor would inherit $1,000 – with an equal amount going to Trueblood. And by August 1915, the couple was $2,000 richer. Edward Dooley had fallen ill and had died after just a few days – typhoid, the doctors said.

"There was nothing suspicious about the death," Matthews said. "It was ruled as food poisoning or typhoid."

As Edward lay dying, Trueblood convinced her husband to revise his insurance policy – for the family's protection, she argued. A new policy was drafted for Robert and his wife, stating that if either died, the surviving spouse would receive $2,000.

Just one month later, Robert Dooley followed in his brother's footsteps – succumbing to typhoid in a similar fashion. Trueblood, however, had begun to build herself a substantial nest egg. Only six weeks after losing her husband, Trueblood's infant daughter, Laura Marie, "drank from a contaminated well," according to reports – leaving the widow lonely and desperate for companionship.

Since accidental poisonings did occasionally occur in rural areas, and epidemics – particularly typhoid – were rampant during that time, the deaths of the Dooleys were only briefly investigated by authorities.

"Little children died all the time, at that period of history," Matthews said. "She probably got a lot of sympathy, 'oh, that poor woman. She's lost her daughter, her husband, all to this stomach flu.'"

Trueblood endured a brief but mandatory period of mourning after losing her family, but soon struck up a relationship with a waiter at her favorite Twin Falls restaurant. William McHaffie married Trueblood just two years after the loss of her first husband and only child, and the couple immediately sought an insurance policy for William. Trueblood was named as William's only beneficiary, to receive $5,000 if anything was to happen to him.

The couple moved to Hardin, Montana, and only a year after they married, William died of "influenza." According to his friends and customers, William had always been a robust, healthy man – and the speed and depth of his sudden illness shocked them.

"Lyda Trublood was very careful," said crime author Diane Fanning. "She waited until they actually got sick – then, it was easier to believe that they had died of an illness. Everybody thought it was something he ate that finally did him in, but all that it was, really, was Lyda Trueblood."

Unfortunately for Trueblood, however, William had failed to pay the second premium on his insurance policy, letting it lapse. Trueblood received nothing for her efforts. Days after her late husband's funeral, Trueblood sold all her property and disappeared.

Moving on

After relocating to Denver, Trueblood managed to ensnare another victim – a farm machinery salesman she had met during her previous marriage to William. In fact, William had told friends that after he'd come to their door in an attempt to make a sale, Trueblood had seemed "struck" by him – and neighbours reported that the happy couple had even started fighting more after that.

Trueblood married Harlan Lewis in March of 1919, and took him with her back to Montana. The couple settled in Billings, and only one month later, Harlan took out a $10,000 life insurance policy. According to Matthews, the larger policies are an indication that

Trueblood was manipulating the men in order to receive greater payouts.

"(Trueblood) was motivated by one thing, and one thing only - greed," said former FBI profiler Candice Delong. "She wanted money."

By mid-July, just three months after the wedding, disaster had struck. After falling ill to a sudden case "ptomaine poisoning," Harlan left Trueblood a widow for the third time – and this time, the cheque came through. After cashing out the estate, Trueblood disappeared again. Instead of heading somewhere new, however, Trueblood decided to return to Idaho.

Under the name of Lyda McHaffie, Trueblood checked into the Rogerson Hotel in Twin Falls in May 1919, and found herself a job at the Grille Café on Main Avenue. Business at the café picked up immediately, reports claim, and the foreman of Ira Perrine's Blue Lake Ranch, Edward Meyer, started visiting the restaurant regularly.

"Folks couldn't help noticing that the air sort of shimmered when (Trueblood's) eyes met Ed's," wrote Jaffe in his profile. "And that the ham he got was thicker, the eggs sunnier than those served other patrons."

The very next month, Trueblood moved to Pocatello, Idaho, where she married Edward Meyer and settled on a ranch.

"She rigged herself out fit to kill, bought a long mink coat and a closed car. Everybody in town was talking about the way she ran around to dances," said Ormsby. "She talked around town that she wasn't in love with Ed, but she wanted a home, and she said that sometime she might learn to love him."

Although she had started going by the name "Anna McHaffie," Trueblood showed no other signs of leaving her past life behind her. She applied for an insurance policy in Edward's name the day after the wedding, in the amount of $10,000 – however, the policy was not approved, and reasons were never clarified. It's possible that insurance companies were beginning to wise up to the run of bad luck Trueblood had encountered.

Suspicious situation

Only two weeks after the couple had wed, on August 25, Edward took ill. Doctors at the hospital claimed he had an excellent chance of recovery, but he was dead by September 7.

"She didn't wait for him to get sick," said Matthews. "Maybe she grew impatient, and that was probably the mistake she made in all of this."

Trueblood's previous husbands had been fairly low-key, unlikely to attract attention despite the unbelievable series of coincidences that had resulted in their deaths – and Trueblood's subsequent insurance claims. Edward Meyer, however, was a different case. As a prominent figure in Twin Falls, Edward had dealings with many of the leading business and farm people in the region – including the Twin Falls county sheriff.

"The townsfolk weren't just satisfied," Ormsby said. "They started a lot of talk, and the insurance company held up payment on the policy. The matter got into politics and folks wanted to know what the candidates for sheriff would do about (Trueblood)."

When traces of arsenic were discovered during a routine post-mortem examination, detectives finally brought the widow in for questioning.

"The investigation was just getting underway when the woman disappeared," stated an article published in the New York Times on May 13, 1921. "Detectives traced her to Los Angeles, and kept track of her while the bodies of the two (Dooleys), the infant daughter, and McHaffie were exhumed and portions of the viscera were sent to chemists."

Edward Meyer's death had become somewhat of a political issue in the 1920 campaign for sheriff, and potential candidates were asked how they planned to handle the case. The current sheriff passed the case to a "remarkable" deputy, Virgin Ormsby – and the investigation would be virtually his only assignment for months.

"After she left for California, the town got more dissatisfied than ever, and in January, I was assigned to the case," Ormsby said. "I've had the bodies of the men dissatisfied and examined – three chemists each working separately reported to me that they found arsenic. I interviewed the doctors who attended the husbands and obtained statements from them that enabled me to build a strong case against her."

Ormsby even discovered that a relative of Trueblood's first husband and brother-in-law had been studying the suspicious deaths in his family. A chemist named Earl Dooley had already begun to consider the possibility that Robert and Edward Dooley had been poisoned with arsenic – and according to Fanning, his suspicions led him to investigate the scene of Trueblood's most recent victim.

After taking samples from Edward Meyer's vomit in the sand, Earl had them tested.

"Sure enough, he found arsenic – and when that happened, he went to a doctor to get it confirmed in another lab," Fanning said. "It was definitely arsenic."

Mounting evidence

Police first determined that the Dooley brothers had been poisoned, as well as Trueblood's own child. Officers in Montana started investigating the cases of Harlan Lewis and William McHaffie, intrigued by the seemingly impossible coincidences that had led Trueblood to make so many insurance claims. Trueblood, meanwhile, was busy seducing her fifth husband, Paul Southard, in Los Angeles – while prosecutor Frank L. Stephen started building a case against her back in Twin Falls.

While working odd jobs, saving her money, and reportedly describing herself as a nurse, Trueblood managed to convince Paul to propose. The two were married in November of 1920. Although Paul, who served as a seaman in the navy, claimed he needed no additional insurance coverage beyond typical provisions, Ormsby learned that a policy had in fact been taken out on Chief Petty Officer Paul Southard – with Trueblood named as the beneficiary.

Shortly after they were wed, Paul was transferred from Los Angeles to Pearl Harbour, and his new bride joined him in Hawaii. Ormsby was in hot pursuit, having tracked Trueblood with the help of California law enforcement. Officers in Honolulu received a warrant for Trueblood's arrest in May 1921. She was picked up on May 12 to return to Boise, Idaho, for her trial – with her husband Paul at her side.

"She's been a mighty good wife to me," said Paul, who refused to believe the charges, "and I don't care if she married ten men before, and they all died. That wouldn't make her a murderess."

Although tabloids had already started running headlines about the gruesome tale, labelling Trueblood catchy names like "Lethal Lyda" or "The Arsenic Widow," Trueblood maintained her innocence as she and Paul prepared to catch the *Matsonia* out of Honolulu. Some reports claimed she was acting "like any lucky vacationer about to embark on an ocean cruise," her neck heavy with flowered leis.

"I am entirely innocent, and I look forward to the trip with optimism," Trueblood said in a brief statement to the press. "I am anxious to get back to Twin Falls and face my accusers."

At the jail, Trueblood finally granted an interview to reporter Hazel Pedlar Faulkner, with the San Francisco Examiner. Pedlar Faulkner described the accused as "dainty, friendly, and refined" – not exactly the picture of a "sinister murderer," she said.

"I have been nervous because of my imprisonment and the unnecessary disgrace to my husband," Pedlar Faulkner quotes Trueblood as saying. "I know as well as anything that I can clear myself. The evidence gathered against me is purely circumstantial. Their work is to prove the charges, and that will not be easy because of the documents I hold."

Trueblood claimed that her husbands had died because she was a "typhoid carrier," and even stated that she had nothing to do with the large life insurance policies her late husbands had all secured before their untimely deaths.

"Life insurance was no object to me," stated Trueblood in Pedlar Faulkner's interview. "I have had enough money. And what insurance my husbands carried were business propositions they took out without regard to me or without consulting me, generally."

Before leaving San Francisco to bring Trueblood back to Boise, Ormsby and his wife, Nellie, took the accused for one last night on the town. After having dinner at a restaurant and strolling through a downtown shopping district, the Ormsbys and their charge attended a vaudeville show at the Orpheum Theatre.

Although Trueblood was trying to remain under the radar, a San Francisco Chronicle reporter recognized her – and wrote about her activities the next morning.

"With the grim specters of four dead husbands, a brother-in-law, and her infant baby hovering near her, while the accusing finger of the law points at her and charges murder, Mrs. Lyda Eva Southard, psychological enigma, calmly spent yesterday seeing the sights of San Francisco," read Herb Westen's article in the San Francisco Call and Post.

"She smiles, a trifle shyly perhaps, but a bored light creeps around her eyes as if to her it is all a tedious legal jumble, which will steal precious hours from her pursuit of happiness."

Up to the jury

Despite Trueblood's denial of the charges, the state contended that she'd fed Edward Meyer, her fourth husband, hefty doses of arsenic extracted from flypaper. Trueblood denied it and the state presented further evidence – largely circumstantial, but it was still enough for a conviction.

The trial, which started on October 3 and lasted six weeks, received attention nation-wide. At the time, it would become the longest criminal trial in history. Witnesses were called from Missouri, Montana, Tennessee, and California – a total of 182 named to appear, but not all were called to the stand.

Prosecutor Stephen tried desperately to bring in Buddy Thornberg to testify against Trueblood – a reporter for the Daily News in Twin Falls who had come close to marrying Trueblood shortly before she snagged Edward Meyer. He'd met the widow at the café, and she had swept him off his feet. According to reports, Thornberg had told his friends he would be marrying the "rich widow from Montana," and – on her advice – he was considering taking out an additional private insurance policy on top of the $10,000 government policy he already had in place.

After his friends managed to convince him to not follow through with a marriage, however, Thornberg had ended his relationship with Trueblood and was presumed to have moved to Washington – never to be heard from again.

An article claimed that "every session of the trial found the court auditorium filled to capacity, principally by women and girls." Another report claimed the trail was, "draggy," and "rather technical – arsenic versus typhoid, laboratory tests versus the official death certificate. This certificate, giving typhoid as the cause of death, was more or less (Trueblood's) sole defense."

The whole case presented against Trueblood suggested that she didn't particularly love her husband, and could have – and likely did – poison him. Not only that, she took out insurance on his life, and fled immediately after his death.

According to Ormsby, a visit to the McHaffies' home in Montana had uncovered evidence to back up this theory. He'd discovered a "large quantity" of cut-up flypaper containing arsenic in the basement, with residue of arsenic in a pot Trueblood had likely used to boil the poison out – before serving it to her husband in tainted food.

"(Trueblood) went about her killing very deliberately," Fanning said. "She bought out everything the store had in flypaper. It was obvious that she wanted to have a permanent supply on hand."

An article published in the New York Times on October 9, 1921 stated that under the questioning of Prosecuting Attorney Frank Stephen, Dr E. F. Roberbaugh, state chemist, confirmed the presence of arsenic poison in the body of Edward Meyer when he examined the body in April of that year.

"The witness testified he found .05 milligrams of poison in five grams of a specimen of several internal organs and .10 milligrams in a ten-gram quantity of the specimen," the article read. "The witness said the distribution of poison throughout the system was not equal and he estimated that a little less than five grains of poison probably was contained in Meyer's body."

He added that the findings "virtually duplicated" those obtained immediately after Edward Meyer's death in September, 1920.

The state requested permission to introduce further evidence relating to the deaths of Trueblood's other husbands, and the judge ruled the testimony admissible. While physicians did, in some instances, contradict testimony of other expert witnesses on the question of cause of death, analysis made by three separate chemists agreed that poison was present in all bodies exhumed.

"She poisoned their food, and over time, the arsenic would build up," said Fanning. "Most of the death certificates all said some sort of stomach ailment."

After a deliberation of twenty-three hours, the jury came back with a verdict on November 4, 1921. Trueblood was found guilty of second-degree murder. Speculation was that the jury had "blanched" at the thought of hanging a woman, but there was no doubt that she had done it. Even her husband, Paul Southard, filed for divorce after watching the trial.

"Lyda Trueblood was a classic black widow," Delong said. "And she did it for money."

According to an article in the November 5, 1921 issue of the Sacramento Union, Trueblood showed "no sign of feeling," and didn't even raise her eyes from the floor as the verdict was read. This was typical of Trueblood's attitude throughout the trial, however.

"On the stand, the accused woman maintained an unperturbed attitude throughout a long grilling by the prosecution, which failed to adduce any important admissions from her," the article stated.

Only eight years after Trueblood's incarceration, Ormsby suffered a paralytic stroke and died in his wife's arms. His obituary ran on the front page of the December 30, 1929 edition of the Twin Falls Times – and flowers were delivered to his funeral, sent from a Lyda Southard.

A "break for freedom"

Still, the guilty verdict and the sentence of at least ten years in prison wasn't enough to keep Trueblood from seducing men.

"She proved that no prison walls can hold her, and made her escape from the Idaho State Penitentiary by fascinating, as did Milady, a prison guard, who is believed to have rigged up for her an ingenious ladder of plumbers' pipes and torn blankets and garden hose," read an article published in the October 25, 1931 issue of the Salt Lake Tribune. "This guard, however, died before (Trueblood) made her break for freedom."

According to the article, Trueblood had already served ten years of her sentence and was eligible for parole when she made her great escape on May 4, 1931. The ladder, fashioned for her by prison guard Jack Watkins, had been buried for months beneath the prison walls. Watkins had also provided Trueblood with a saw, which she used to remove a bar from her cell window.

"The escape itself was dramatic," the article continued. "Women inmates, evidently under the spell of the woman, who could fascinate those of her own sex as well as men, staged a party and played the phonograph and sang while she was gaining her way to liberty."

Trueblood ran right into the arms of David Minton. Minton, an ex-convict himself, had fallen under Trueblood's spell while he was still behind bars. After he helped Trueblood escape from prison, she'd ended the relationship. Leaving him alive was a mistake, however – enraged, Minton went to the police and told them they could find Trueblood in Topeka, Kansas.

This, however, was not before a nation-wide manhunt was organized to attempt to locate Trueblood, who was described by Warden R. E. Thomas of the Idaho State Penitentiary as "one of the most dangerous criminals at large."

"Some man will probably pay with his life in agony and death before this ruthless woman can again be brought to justice," he said. "That she is the modern 'Mrs. Bluebeard' is certain."

In fact, before the police found her in Kansas, Trueblood had managed to swindle another man into marrying her. Harry Whitlock, who later described Trueblood as a "model wife," was shocked when the police showed up looking for her. The relationship had begun when Trueblood, calling herself "Fern," had started doing housekeeping work for Whitlock – and she had suggested he take out a $20,000 life insurance policy, but it hadn't been purchased before she asked him for some travel money and took off.

Fifteen months after her escape, Trueblood was returned to Boise – with her marriage to Whitlock annulled.

Back in prison, Trueblood continued to seduce her prey. This time, she set her sights on George Rudd, a prison warden. She managed to convince him to grant her special privileges – frequent day trip to a local resort, visitation to see her sick mother, and even transportation to Boise to see movies. However, when authorities discovered that he'd been treating Trueblood to these privileges, Rudd was forced to resign from his position.

Free at last

Finally, Trueblood was paroled from prison on October 3, 1941, and fully pardoned only one year later.

"I think they figured that she had lost most of her good looks and charm, and was no longer a menace to society," Matthews said.

After spending a few years living with her sister, Blanche Quigley, in Nyssa, Oregon, Trueblood returned to her family's farm at Twin Falls – but the local townspeople and even her relatives weren't pleased to see her.

A few months later, Trueblood left for Provo, Utah, where no one knew her, and pulled together the funds to purchase a small secondhand shop. There, she married her seventh husband, Hal Shaw. However, once Shaw's children discovered who she was and learned about her unsavory past, he vanished – leaving her to move to Salt Lake City, where she worked for several years as a housekeeper and waitress.

"You wonder, did (the husbands) ever suspect that it was not a natural illness that was making them suffer in agony," Fanning said. "We can only hope that they never understood what was really happening."

Trueblood died of a heart attack on February 5, 1958 in Salt Lake City. Her body remains at Sunset Memorial Park in Twin Falls, Idaho, where she was buried as Anna E. Shaw. Still, some report seeing a ghost bearing Trueblood's likeness haunting the halls of the Idaho prison to this day – the prison's most notorious inmate, maintaining a presence even after her death.

"When she finally died, it was from a heart attack," Fanning said. "It's amazing to think that (Trueblood) actually had a heart."

BLACK WIDOW : THE TRUE STORY OF MARGARET RUDIN

BRIANNA VALDES

Margaret Rudin, dubbed the Black Widow of Las Vegas, went on trial on February 26, 2001 for the murder of her fifth husband, real estate king Ronald Rudin. After a lengthy, chaotic trial and her defense claiming that involvement in illegal activities resulted in Ron's death, the jury found her guilty on May 2, 2001. In August, the court sentenced Margaret Rudin to life in prison with the possibility of parole in 20 years.

According to reports, Ron Rudin went missing about a week before Christmas in '94. He paid a visit to wife Margaret Rudin's antique shop, in the same plaza as his real estate business. Officials said that Margaret Rudin did not report Ron missing until a few days after he disappeared. She told police she thought nothing of it at first because, aside from Ron being upset with her after an argument, he seemed like his usual self.

About a month after Ron disappeared, a couple of civilians stumbled upon human remain near Lake Mohave in Nevada. Police found ashes and fragments of bones in the burn pile. However, the skull, which was inches away, remained mostly intact. It had at least four bullet holes, which forensics later matched to a .22 caliber weapon. Police made two trips to the house, and on the second visit, they found blood on the walls, photographs and items removed from the house including a mattress and carpet. However, though the police suspected that Margaret Rudin killed her husband, the evidence up to that point was circumstantial at best.

A year and a half year later, a diver found a .22 caliber gun with a built-in silencer in Lake Mead. This was the same gun Ron Rudin reported missing about six years before his death. When officials tested the gun in the forensics lab, the ammo matched the rounds found in Ron Rudin's skull. Police determined that the .22 was the murder weapon, and, with this new piece of evidence added to the other circumstantial clues they had, charged Margaret Rudin with the murder of her husband. However, Margaret left town before they indicted and arrested her, and she stayed out of sight for over two years.

Almost a year after the diver found the gun that allegedly killed Ron Rudin, police finally indicted Margaret Rudin.

Authorities finally apprehended Margaret Rudin in 1999. Someone who saw her picture and story on the T.V. show "America's Most Wanted" called and reported seeing her in a small town in Massachusetts.

Police used a pizza delivery person to help them capture Margaret. They borrowed the person's uniform and an empty pizza box, and barged in the house when her male companion opened the door. According to some reports, they found her cowering in the bathroom.

Margaret Rudin was born Margaret Lee Frost in Memphis, Tennessee on May 31, 1943. She said that she and her family never lived in one place for very long, and that she and her two sisters constantly changed schools.

"I didn't grow up any place. We were constantly moving, you know, like, I transferred schools 22 different times, um, before I graduated high school. I lived in 15 states in 15 years. I never had a hometown."

Margaret said that her father was strict and dominating, and that he rarely showed affection to her or her sisters.

Both Margaret and Ron were married four times before they met at the First Church of Religious Science in Las Vegas. They married on September 11, 1987.

Margaret's mother, Eloise Frost, stood behind her daughter throughout the entire trial. She never believed Margaret capable of murder.

"I want to live long enough to see Margaret pronounced innocent, because she is innocent."

Margaret Rudin's daughter, Kristina Mason firmly believed that her mother was innocent. She said her childhood was a good one, and that the mother with whom she grew up was not a murderer.

"She's just a wonderful person and I'm proud to say she's my mother."

The court sentenced Margaret Rudin in September 2001. Although she received life in a medium security facility, plus a year for planting the bugs in her husband's office, they also added that she would be eligible for parole in 2011. She began preparing, and petitioning, for her appeal, carefully heeding the filing deadlines.

80-year-old Eloise cried when Margaret was convicted, saying that now she may never see her daughter again.

Kristina Mason burst into tears.

"I'm so disappointed."

Ronald Rudin seemed to predict his own death, or at least his murder. Months before he went missing, he had his will changed, with specific instructions for investigators to follow in the event that he died under suspicious circumstances.

"In the event my death is caused by violent means [for example gunshot, knife or a violent automobile accident] extraordinary steps be taken in investigating the true cause of the death. Should said death be caused directly or indirectly by a beneficiary of my estate, said beneficiary shall be totally excluded from my estate and/or any trusts I may have in existence."

Although most of Nevada's case against Margaret was circumstantial, authorities say there were a few things that seemed suspicious to them from the beginning. First, Margaret herself admitted that her marriage to Ron was less than ideal. She told police that they often argued about her work schedule. Later, when authorities discovered that she had planted listening devices in Ron Rudin's home office, she also admitted that she suspected that Ron was having an affair, and upon eavesdropping on a phone conversation, discovered proof to back her suspicions.

Jimmy Vacarro, a Vegas detective, confirmed that the Las Vegas police believed without a doubt that Margaret Rudin was responsible for Ron's murder.

"We know there was this real rocky roller-coaster relationship between Margaret Rudin and her husband... [It took] Margaret two days to file a missing persons report and that she did so only after Ron's coworkers informed police first...Generally speaking, the spouse is missing, the wife's the one reporting it."

Second, officials say that Margaret waited a few days before reporting Ron missing, even though his employees at his real estate company were concerned and investigating as soon as he did not show up that Monday morning.

Margaret Rudin offered a logical explanation to her hesitation to bring in police. She said she thought little of it at first because they had another fight and he left angry, which was common for Ron. She also said that, aside from Ron being upset with her after an argument, he seemed like his usual self.

"He seemed ok. He does not seem upset. He had, had been a little peeved at me over the weekend because I had to work all the time... "Well, I thought nothing of it because, you know, maybe he did get peeved... and maybe he did decide to go out for awhile... maybe he did go to, you know... wherever."

Margaret made a point of mentioning her previous marriages in one of her interviews.

"I don't have a history of staying with somebody if I'm really unhappy. I have a history of divorcing... There was problems. He was a difficult person at times, but yes, I did love him..."

Margaret said Ron also drank quite a bit after just a few months of marriage. However, she told reporters that she was not mad about the alcohol or the other women, even when Su Lyles, a close friend and a former employee of Mr. Rudin's, testified that in the fall of 1993, their relationship became more intimate. At least twice, she said, they had discussed their feelings for each other over the telephone during calls made from his office.

"You know why? It is because 99 percent of the men that I have ever had in my life had affairs. Ninety percent of men do, you might as well expect it."

Margaret admitted that, although the affairs wounded her, she loved her husband and desperately wanted to work out things with him.

Police grew even more suspicious when they discovered that Margaret hired a man named Augustine Lovato to help her remove some dirty carpet and furniture from the master bedroom. She then renovated the bedroom she shared with her husband into an office while Ron was still missing.

Lovato testified that the mattress and carpet he removed from the Rudin's home had suspicious brown stains on it and a strong odor that alarmed him.

"It didn't seem right, him still being missing and me turning their master bedroom into an office and then those splatters on that picture. Like I got the heebie-jeebies."

Lovato also claimed that he heard a strange sound in the bathtub in the master bathroom. He said that, upon inspection, it looked about the same color and consistency as the stains on the mattress and carpet he removed.

The same day he moved the allegedly bloodstained items from the Rudin's bedroom, Margaret Rudin asked Lovato to mail a package addressed to her mother. Lovato claimed that he forgot to mail the package, and ultimately turned it over to the police. After obtaining a search warrant, police opened the package and discovered several personal items inside, including a postcard from Israel signed "Love, Yehuda," a photo of Yehuda Sharon, the man with whom police suspected that Margaret Rudin was having an affair, and a handwritten letter from Rudin to her mother containing the message, "Please hold on to my Ye."

Attorneys discovered later that Lovato reported all these mysterious findings after Ron Rudin's other trustees announced their reward for information about Ron's disappearance. However, Lovato argued that he cooperated with police before anyone told him there was a reward, which Ron's trustees did grant him.

The most suspicious thing that Margaret Rudin did, according to police, was going on the run before the state served her with her indictment. Investigators believed that, if Margaret were innocent, she would not have fled. However, Margaret says that she ran out of fear, not guilt.

"[I ran] because I was afraid of being found by Ron's shadowy business associates... It was difficult. I was always looking over my shoulder. I was always afraid, I was afraid of who stood to gain the most, you know, from Ron's murder."

During the trial, the state also used the testimony of almost 70 witnesses, including Yehuda Sharon and Margaret's sister, Donna Cantrell. Prosecutors granted Yehuda Sharon total immunity in exchange for his testimony against Margaret Rudin. However, when he took the stand, he not only had little to say regarding Margaret's guilt, he denied aiding her in disposing of Ron Rudin's remains. He told the court that he rented a van, planning to make a trip from Vegas to California for his business on the night in question. However, he said that he only made it half way there and then turned around due to unexpected weather conditions. Furthermore, his destination was the opposite direction from the place where officials found Ron Rudin's remains. Once the prosecution determined that Margaret's friend, Yehuda Sharon, was likely not an accomplice to Ron's murder, no other suspects were detained or questions, and most people assumed that Margaret had somehow dismembered her husband's body, put it in the heavy steamer trunk and hauled it out to the desert all by herself.

Cantrell testified that she was aware of her sister's marital problems. She said that Margaret had spoken to her many times about Ron's drinking and her suspicions about his involvement with other women. She made comments on Rudin's restless desire to get away from Ron.

"I said, 'I thought you were going to divorce him,' and she said, 'He's not in very good health. He can't even walk without being out of breath, and I think I'll wait.' [Margaret told me] to tell [police] that she and Ron were getting along better than ever. And that the girlfriend wasn't an issue. [I don't] think that this statement would have been true."

Despite the authorities' strong belief that she murdered her husband, Margaret Rudin maintained her innocents. In interviews after the trial and her conviction, she states repeatedly that she loved her husband and could never kill him. She suggested that there might be another motive for her husband's murder.

"Nobody knows the whole Ron. That's the part that worries me. Maybe there's something that was going on with a business or a personal deal."

Margaret also suspected that someone knew more than they told detectives.

"I think that there are people that know things. I think that there are people who haven't come forth before. Maybe they didn't know how, maybe they were afraid, maybe they were intimidated."

Margaret Rudin's trial was rocky from the beginning. One of her defense attorneys, Michael Amador, started with an opening statement, which consisted of nothing but a long, irrelevant, self-based speech.

"This is a great day, in a lot of different ways. Some days are difficult; some days we hear bad news or we go through a difficult time, but every day, every day, depending on how you look at it, with a few exceptions, can be a celebration.

This is a great today for me. This is a culmination of a career. The people in this case, we are not strangers; we know each other. Chris and I were sworn in as deputy DAs the same day. And I congratulate Chris on a presentation that was organized and well thought out, the best money can buy. It was really good.

If you want to know an opinion about me, I guarantee you'll find some, different ones from different people. Not many people know me. I have few close friends, like Ronald Rudin had few close friends.

I could be a wonderful, caring father, coaching soccer, helping kids with their homework, which I did the first time I got married when they were young.

Then another day, I might scream at someone, yell at them for-I don't know-for asking me some question, because I was too busy and I was thinking of something else.

The difficulty I have at times is communicating to people. I have to look at it and talk to other people and they will bring me back down to earth and say, Mike, what are you trying to say? What are you trying to get across?"

Amador also made a strange, challenging statement.

"During the course of the trial, there may be objections and things like that. Don't worry about it."

Judge Joseph Bonaventure cut off Amador's speech.

"I don't know what that means: Don't worry about objections. We have to do other things. I have no idea what that means. If there's an objection, I'm either going to overrule it or sustain it and that's the law...

I keep saying this-and I let you get away with a lot, Mr. Amador-but the purpose for an opening statement is just to indicate what the evidence is going to tend to show and not go into your personal beliefs and your passion and soccer dad and yelling at the staff and whether you were a green lawyer and know all the cops and used to be a D.A. and you communicate differently. I never heard that in [an] opening statement in my life."

During the opening statements, the State quoted a portion of Margaret Rudin's diary.

"My life has always been unique, exciting, full of change, challenges and stimulus and full of interesting casts of characters and that is okay.

It just is, and I accept that for my past, but I know that, by programming my mind, I can now redirect any future stage plays and pick my own screen play and cast, because I am the producer, director and star of any and all new plays on my stage called life.

I've always vaguely known these facts and lived my life accordingly, but I never realized what control-I never realized what control I could have over every segment of this one time stage production called "Margaret's Life.""

Amador did a curious thing at the trial. He employed a makeup artist from a professional modeling agency and paid almost $500 an hour, out of his own pocket, to make Margaret appear worn, delicate, and tired.

Amador got under Judge Bonaventure's skin by repeatedly being late to appear in court, questionable forms he submitted, and his cell phone, which he never turned off or down during the trial. Rumors eventually spread that Amador was using drugs, drinking and partying all night long when he had to be in court early the next morning.

Rumors circulated that Amador was also behaving inappropriately with Margaret Rudin's belongings and private, confidential information. Amador hired a new office assistant named Annie Jackson during the proceedings for the Rudin trial. She revealed information regarding some of the rumors about Amador.

"There is no other way to say the following: when Mr. Amador told the court that he did not have any book or movie contracts, he was lying. Michael Amador does have book contracts and movie contracts regarding the Margaret Rudin case. When we returned to the office after Mr. Amador made those false representations to the court, he asked me to grab all of the contracts so that he could put them in his little safe in the back closet. He told me, "I don't want anyone to find out that I have these, then I'm sure they'll be investigating and looking for these."

Margaret asked early on for an even amount of participation from her attorneys. She asked that Thomas Pitaro take a more active role in the proceedings, because she did not believe that Michael Amador was properly prepared.

"We haven't even subpoenaed my witnesses yet. And I'm getting so nervous. I mean, I'm getting panicky."

Pitaro agreed after warning the judge that, although he would do his best, he was uncertain if he would be able to uphold that bargain throughout the entire trial.

Throughout all the chaos in the Rudin trial, one juror believed Margaret's side of the story. During the first couple of days of deliberation, she held fast to her opinion that Margaret did not kill Ron. However, hours before the foreperson read the jury's verdict, juror #11 changed her vote. She was distraught, wiping her eyes with a napkin. She hesitated before replying with a hushed "Yes" when the court asked her if the verdict was, in fact, hers, too.

Even though the verdict was ultimately unanimous, the juror cried as she apologized to Rudin when the foreperson read the jury's verdict.

During the time before she opted to vote Margaret Rudin guilty, juror #11 faced allegations from her peers of choosing not to join the deliberation efforts, lying, and calling one of the jury substitutes with her concerns about the case. Amador said he thought the juror was possibly "brow-beaten" into changing her vote.

Foreperson for the Rudin case's jury, Ronald Vest, said that no one "twisted her arm."

"We didn't bribe her or threaten her. She came to this on her own."

Vest believed that Rudin's was an open and shut case.

"Rudin's guilt was clear early on. [The defense's case was] a waste of time... [Amador was] bordering on incompetent... [The guilty verdict was a] slam dunk with a stepladder... I didn't buy any of it. I don't think any of us bought any of the defense case. The mountain of evidence had 11 of the jurors ready to convict as early as Thursday, but one person from the beginning did not see it that way... juror #11 seemed so bent on acquitting Rudin that [I] began to wonder if she had been bribed or threatened or simply wanted attention. [I] confronted her about [my] suspicions, and she denied them. There was a little bit of swearing. It was fast and furious but we hashed it out."

Vest admitted that he had had to request substitutes on a few occasions, because his special needs students were struggling in class without him. He believed that, had he not been there, they would not have been able to replace him.

"Six substitutes, three of which said they would never come back and one who just sat at the desk shaking like he was scared... my principal said, Well, maybe there's some reason why you need to be on this jury."

The judge in the Rudin trial met with the hesitant juror privately, in his chambers, to address her contact, and discussion about case-related information, with an alternate juror. Whenever Margaret Rudin's defense team broached the subject, the court dismissed it, stating that it had little impact on the outcome of the trial.

Margaret Rudin's conviction shocked Amador. He spoke with disdain about the prosecutors. He could not believe that the prosecutors successfully sold their case.

"If you have any understanding of psychology, history, or criminology, women don't do that, men do," said Amador. "That kind of mutilation is done by men over money or, in rare cases, serial killers. Women don't even order stuff like that—they want it clean... [The prosecutors] make me sick... I don't know how it is that right-thinking people can find someone guilty with no evidence."

Rudin had requested a mistrial due to Amador's antics and all the dissention with the jury. Pitaro led the defense team at the motion, hoping to prove that Amador was ill prepared for the case and not behaving with appropriate competence as an attorney.

"The fundamental problem that we have is this case is not ready to go to trial. For whatever reason it's not ready, it's not ready. That's obvious to any observer of this case, that for the first two weeks this is not the way you try cases and this is not the way you try murder cases. And what we are putting on in front of the world is a farce, and that disturbs me as an attorney. [T]his has become a sham, a farce and a mockery."

The State expressed similar concerns.

"Already we have an appellate issue now, should they have hired a forensic accountant. And I mean they came into this thing hiring their experts two weeks before the trial and they didn't start looking at the evidence until the day of trial. Two days into it, we still don't have reports back for most of them... Mr. Pitaro is coming in now, he's going to try to read the stuff and catch up. He already feels there's certain things that should have happened that didn't happen. All I can say is we're really uncomfortable with the record here."

The district court, however, was hesitant to declare a mistrial because of the double jeopardy laws. As it turned out, those did not apply in Margaret Rudin's case.

Amador stood with Margaret Rudin and the rest of her defense team during the motion for mistrial. However, when the prosecutors submitted documentation regarding his ineffectiveness, he contradicted himself.

"Nobody worked harder or spent more time before or during the Rudin trial nor knew the case better than I... [I] spend many hours on the case, from the time [I] took it in August of 2000 and [my] vacation in November 2000... [I] filed at least 24 motions and investigated all major witnesses in the case and organized their files prior to the vacation."

The defense also argued that improper communication took place between the judge, juror 11 and the alternate, which tainted the jury. According to the alternate, juror 11 called the alternate, saying she was upset because she was the only person in favor of a not guilty verdict and because she had gotten into an altercation with the staff person at a restaurant during a recess. After questioning the alternate and the juror in the presence of the State and the defense, the district court denied Rudin's motion for a mistrial. The district court also chose not to replace the juror. They concluded that neither the jury nor Rudin's case were compromised.

The court removed Amador from Margaret Rudin's case, but rejected her request for a mistrial. The judge almost immediately disregarded Margaret's mistrial motion.

"[Rudin] failed to present any specific argument to support a determination that she has been prejudiced. [The] affidavits are legally insufficient, as conclusions, rumors, beliefs, and opinions are not sufficient to form a basis for a new trial... As to Mr. Amador's personal antics which the defense seems to harp upon as tantalizing tidbits, this court feels it is not honorable to kick a man when he is down as the record speaks for itself. Rudin, at taxpayer expense, also had at her side criminal defense attorneys Thomas Pitaro and John Momot."

Bonaventure was biased, blunt, and cold at Margaret's sentencing hearing, just as he was throughout the entire trial.

"You're going to be locked away in the cold confines of your prison cell, never to be heard from again."

Although she received life in a medium security facility, plus a year for planting the bugs in her husband's office, they also added that she would be eligible for parole in 2011. She began preparing, and petitioning, for her appeal, carefully heeding the filing deadlines.

The appeals court believed that one of Margaret Rudin's former attorneys, Dayvid Figler, was responsible for her initial petitions for appeal. Figler denied any wrongdoing, and said that, although he was not at fault, she did deserve a shot at a new trial.

"I didn't screw up her trial. I didn't screw up her appeal. The court was giving extra time to get this very burdensome case before it. Everyone was operating under the assumption that she had more time to file the post-conviction appeal."

Figler called Rudin's appeal a "very complicated, burdensome, voluminous case" and said that after he took it on, the trial judge granted him extra time because the case was so complex.

Christopher Oram, the lawyer who represented Margaret Rudin during her recent appeal for a new trial, was thrilled with the opportunity.

"She is absolutely innocent. We've been working to prove it for a long time. I'm trying to reverse 10 years of complex litigation that was very unfair... I believe in her innocence. I'm ready to fight, and I wish they would stop playing their games. In the end, get in the ring and fight."

The Ninth Circuit Court of Appeals said that a technicality should not hinder Margaret Rudin's attempt to prove that a lawyer at her original trial ineffectually proved her case. Judge Mary Murguia believed that Figler did not serve Margaret to the best of his ability.

"While Figler regularly attended the court's status hearings, he appears to have done nothing else in support of his client's request for post-conviction relief. [Figler had the case for 645 days] and during that time, [he] had filed nothing in either state or federal court."

In 2007, Oram filed the first and only petition for post-conviction relief, according to Murguia.

Sally Loehrer, a district judge, ruled in 2008 that Michael Amador's performance did constitute as ineffectual in her original trial, and as a result, Margaret Rudin was entitled to a new trial.

"[It was a] case laced with intrigue and spins and loops involving a cast of characters and witnesses [that seemed to have] a lot of ulterior motives."

However, two years later, the Supreme Court overruled, stating that there was not enough evidence to sustain the order.

The Ninth Circuit Court reviewed all the evidence from the original trial, as well as Margaret Rudin's complaints, and her defense team's strategies. They do not believe that all defense attorneys adequately represent their clients just because they participate in every aspect of the trial. They made mention of evidence that was not previously mentioned.

"Sometime during the trial, the defense team located the person who sold the trunk to Rudin and established that it was not a large humpback trunk, but one that was much too small to fit a corpse inside. The defense also located Barbara Orcutt, who indicated that Rudin was indeed concerned about Ron's disappearance and had asked her right after his disappearance to organize a search in the Mt. Charleston area, where she believed Ron might have been. The State apparently had this information, but did not share it with the defense. It is unrealistic to think that the jurors could have put out of their minds all the evidence and adverse events, including the continual admonishment of defense counsel by the district court judge; the bizarre opening statement; the constant continuances and delays throughout the trial, which I am sure were held against the defense; and the belated presentation of important evidence. These harmful events resulted from Amador's conflict of interest and lack of preparation and now require reversal of this case... The evidence certainly indicated that Amador secured media rights while representing Rudin, which was a violation of the Nevada Rules of Professional Conduct.9...Amador was clearly more interested in obtaining information for his book and getting media attention than in developing Rudin's defense."

They also noted the testimony from Annie Jackson, Amador's assistant, and found new information there, as well. Jackson claimed that Amador did not turn over several of Rudin's files, containing diaries, witness statements, and pictures, to the public defender's office because he thought he might need the information in the future.

"I believe there is sufficient evidence in the record, without the necessity of post-trial proceedings, to establish that the defense was totally unprepared to try this case and that Amador had a substantial conflict of interest with his client. This was prejudicial to Rudin, and the result reached was unreliable."

Margaret appeals to the public in a letter she wrote from the Florence McClure Women's Correctional Center.

"The new trial I won [on] March 10, 2015, in the Ninth Circuit Court of Appeals has been blocked by the new NV Attorney General. Next week, their writ to the U.S. Supreme court will be filed."

She explains that, if her case lands in the 99% that skip review this session, it will return to the Ninth Circuit. Since they have already voted in her favor before, she hopes that once again, the NCCA will find her worthy of a new trial, and that this time their decision will be permanent. She maintains her innocence, and she continues to push for her appeal, and her opportunity to have her side of the story told.

HUSBAND KILLER MICHELLE REYNOLDS

GARY GUIDEN

On July 5th, 2004, a Frito Lay delivery pulled into the empty parking lot of a distribution center in Rome, Georgia. The man noticed that another man- one he didn't recognize- was coming out of the office, and although someone in the office in the early morning hours wasn't unusual, not recognizing the man was. According to the diver, the man who came into view appeared to be nervous- looking over his shoulder, glancing around, and checking behind him.

The man, possibly unaware of the delivery driver still sitting in his vehicle, exits the building and enters a mini-van after removing his shirt. Thinking this was odd, the delivery driver entered the Frito Lay office only to discover the scene of a horror film.

He discovered the slumped over body of the regional manager, Thad Reynolds, sitting in a pool of his own blood. He called 911 and EMT's and police officers responded within minutes. However, it was too late. Thad Reynolds was dead before anyone arrived.

Ross Cavitt, a reporter at the scene, noted that Reynolds had been stabbed 19 times. Due to the nature of the stab wounds and the amount of blood, it was obvious to Cavitt that there had been a great struggle.

Thad's death sent shock through his community, but hit his church, the Hollywood Baptist, the hardest as Thad and his wife Michelle were well-known within the church community. In her early days, Michelle had been popular in high school and well respected within her community.

Thad, on the other hand, was a dedicated Christian and devoted father to his 4 children, as well as a loving husband to his wife, Michelle. As a young man, Thad had been heavily involved in sports and was popular at his high school.

"He could always make your day better" stated Julie Crumbley about her late friend Thad.

Michelle was a mother of 4 and a likeable person, according to Thad's close friend, Julie Crumbley.

Before becoming a mother, Michelle had worked as an administrative assistant, but had given the job up after giving birth to her first child in 1992. After the couple began to have children, the decision was made that Michelle would be a stay at home mom and raise their children.

In 1995, however, the couple's relationship took a turn for the worse and Michelle asked for a divorce. Thad's sister, Beverly Owners, claims that Michelle hadn't been happy just being a mother and a wife. It's been said that Michelle had made the following comment to a pastor at the couple's church: "You put your wife on a pedestal, but Thad never put me on a pedestal."

Thad agreed to the divorce, but regretted his decision as he didn't believe in divorce or broken homes. Undone by the divorce, Thad turned to his church for help. Two years after their divorce, the couple remarried, built a new home, and added more children to their family.

Thad's career began to flourish, after he was hired into the Frito Lay company where he was able to work his way to district manager. He also sang in the church's choir and served as a deacon, as well as helped other couples with marriage counseling.

"They appeared to be the most perfect family whenever you would see them" says Crumbley.

Thad's mother told Dateline that the couple had been called Barbie and Ken because of how well their life seemed to be going.

Both Michelle and Thad had a passion for children and worked with the church's youth group to put on shows, skits, and performances in various locations. They worked closely with the church's youth minister, Scott Harper and his wife, Paige. Thad and Scott became best friends and the families became joined at the hip. Paige and Michelle also became close, bonding over their stay at home lifestyles and busy husbands.

So, what went wrong? The answer to this was revealed only after a shocking truth involving Michelle and her best friend's husband came to light.

In 2004, Thad decided to become a minister, as he felt that God was calling to him to join the ministry. In June of that year, Michelle signed up to help the Harper family with a youth retreat, but called Paige shortly before they were set to leave and said that she had had a change of heart.

"She called me last minute and said that she was going to book her own room and was not going to room with me, because she needed her own time" says Paige, when asked about the phone call. This meant that Michelle would be the only chaperon who had her own private room.

"Michelle was distant. She wouldn't speak to me or look me in the eye" Paige says. Paige grew concerned and confronted her best friend. "I said "Michelle is there something wrong? Have I done something to offend you?" and she looked me in the eye and said no, I just want to be around people who are on fire for God."

As her husband prepared to become a minister, Michelle began to spend less time with Paige and more time with her husband, Scott.

"She would constantly be asking him for assistance. More and more she would ask him for help working with the children or how to do certain things with them. They began to email and communicate" says prosecutor, Leigh Patterson.

On Saturday, July 3rd, 2004, the Harper and Reynolds' met up for a long weekend celebration. The next day, a Sunday, the met up once again to attend church together. That day, the families met at a local park to play volleyball, gave snacks, and enjoy each other's company.

"I noticed Michelle being kind of flirtatious towards other men, asking somebody to help her throw a football and stuff like that." Paige says.

"She was a little bit too flirty...wanting other men to pay attention to her" agrees Patterson.

Despite Michelle's odd behavior at the picnic, she and her husband loaded up their children at the end of the evening and went home like nothing had happened.

The next morning Thad left for work before sunrise and while Michelle and the kids were still asleep. After only a few minutes at the office, a van pulled up outside of the office where Thad was working. The driver was Scott Harper, and within a few minutes, Thad would be dead on the floor of his office.

On July 5th, when Thad's body was discovered, the city of Rome, Georgia was thrown into chaos.

The first question on investigator's lips was who would launch a violent attack on the well-loved church deacon?

"There were wounds all over his body, including defensive wounds" says Patterson.

The only witness had been the delivery driver who had discovered Thad's body, but he had been unable to get a good look at Thad's attacker's face or the license plate of the van he had been driving.

Upon investigation of the scene, it became apparent to police that Thad had managed to wound his attacker. This was proved by a large amount of blood that was found by the office doorway- blood that matched up with the delivery driver's statement claiming that the unknown man stopped by the door before getting into his van and leaving the scene.

Also on the scene, police found the empty case for a hunting knife and a pair of glasses. The glasses also matched up with witness testimony, as the man was seen removing his shirt and in doing so, his glasses could have fallen off and been left behind in his haste to get away.

Scott Harper was called to help identify Thad's body and was one of the first people to learn of his death. Scott called his wife and upon hearing the news, Paige become worried about Michelle.

The Harpers drove to the Reynolds house to be with Michelle, however, upon arrival, they found that the church's head pastor was already there.

According to family and friends, Michelle has taken the news stoically.

"You would think that when we got there, Michelle would come and give us a hug or cry and she didn't" said Beverly Owens, surprised at how Michelle took the news.

Thad's mother also noticed Michelle's lack of outward emotion and was concerned by it.

"She had just bought a black dress about two weeks before and made the comment "whoever thought that I'd be using it for this.""

Meanwhile, back at the crime scene, investigators had begun to wonder about Thad's death. To them, it didn't appear to be a random attack and robbery situation, but seemed to have been calculated and planned, as Thad's murderer didn't take any of his money or anything that he had had on him. The reason behind the attack appeared to be one thing: to kill Thad Reynolds.

On the news that evening, a clue was unearthed as to who could have killed the deacon. Scott Roberts, a coworker of Scott Harper, had heard the news asking for leads and picked up the phone almost immediately.

Roberts called the police department and reported to the officials that his coworker, Scott Harper was both friends with Thad and drove a burgundy minivan like the one that had been witnessed leaving the crime scene.

Roberts was asked for a statement and while telling them what he knew, he alerted the police that Scott Harper had been having an affair with someone- information that he claimed he had stumbled upon without meaning to. Roberts worked with phonelines and was tasked with fixing them. A few weeks before the murder, he had tapped into a conversation to fix the phoneline and overheard Harper talking to a woman who wasn't his wife, Paige. He had also overheard that the woman's name was Michelle.

"They were flirting. Lover chit chat, if you will. Kind of reminded me of high school sweethearts" said Roberts in an interview with Dateline.

Officials ended their interview with Roberts by asking a simple question- did Harper wear glasses? Roberts had answered that, yes, Scott Harper did wear glasses.

This left police to wonder were the connections between the van, the glasses, and a possible affair all just coincidence? Or was there something sinister going on?

The Harpers were then brought in for official questioning, where Scott told investigators that he had hurt his hand at the gym, when he was asked why his hand was bandaged. This explained his hand but didn't explain why his glasses were missing.

Scott was released, despite police not believing his story. Paige was starting to doubt her husband, as well.

"When we left the station, I asked him if he knew anything about Thad's murder…about what was going on" Paige said "and he said "do you realize what you're asking me?""

Police obtained a warrant to search Scott's computer at the hospital that he worked at, in hopes of getting answers. They had a particular interest to look into Scott's emails, as they were saved on a public server and could be easily accessed.

It was found that a large portion of the emails were to and from Thad's wife, Michelle. At first, the emails were innocent- mostly consisting of routine topics such as the youth group that Michelle worked with at the church. Gradually, though, the emails became more personal and revealing in nature.

About a month before the death of her husband, the tone of the emails changed.

"She was coming onto him in the emails. Usually under the guise of I know I shouldn't feel this way" Patterson says, referring to Michelle and the emails that she sent to Scott "and he fell for it."

"The emails, especially toward the end, were very graphic and specific" said prosecutor Natalee Staats.

It wasn't clear from the emails when their affair became physical, however, records show that at the youth retreat in June, Scott had booked Michelle's room and stayed in it with her. Paige, although quiet about the whole thing, had noticed Scott get up and leave the room and noted that he didn't return until the next morning.

"He had gone down to Michelle's room and even though they were on a church trip with kids and his wife, and Michelle's daughter there as a participant, they had continued their affair" said Patterson.

Police combed over every detail of their emails, but couldn't decide whether Michelle had coaxed Scott into murdering her husband or not. According to Patterson, Michelle had been very careful with what she said and how she said it.

"Michelle never said "I need you to kill my husband" said Staats. However, she hinted at the idea by sayings things like "You'll have to live longer than Thad for us to be together because he'll never agree to divorce."

After Michelle had planted the idea in Scott's head, he had gone on to lookup poison and arsenic, as well an essay on how to commit the perfect murder Patterson reported.

On the evening of July 4th, hours before the murder would happen, the two exchanged a final round of emails.

"The night before, she tells him what Thad's schedule was going to be the next morning. Specific directions of where he was going to be" she also reports.

"Those were all glaring clues to the police that Michelle might have been involved in a conspiracy to murder her husband" said Staats, in agreeance with Patterson.

Scott had sent Michelle an email giving her an out. The email told Michelle to tell him if she had any hesitations, and that if she did, he wouldn't go through with it. Michelle replied that didn't have any hesitations and was ready for the event to take place.

Scott Harper was charged with murder on July 8th, 2004 after he turned himself in. He was charged with murder, felony murder, aggravated assault, and aggravated battery.

Authorities hoped that Scott would tie Michelle into the case, however, Scott was blinded by his feelings for her and was willing to protect her at all costs. He invoked the right to remain silent and didn't make another statement for or against Michelle's innocence.

Michelle was also arrested, as police had enough evidence from Michelle's own emails, that she had been involved.

"Once they figured it out, they decided pretty quickly that they had enough to charge her as well" said Michelle's attorney, Jim Berry.

An hour or so after Scott had turned himself in, Michelle was placed under arrest and brought into police custody and like her lover, Michelle refused to talk.

"Michelle was arrested as she came out of her attorney's office in downtown Rome" said Patterson.

"I had no clue. Everybody seemed happy" said Paige, who was shocked by the news that Michelle and Scott were in custody.

"Friends that they interacted with at the church didn't dream that the family pastor was having an affair with the deacon's wife" Patterson said.

The fact that Michelle and Scott could and would conspire to murder Thad Reynolds was unthinkable to the members of the church, who knew both people as being kind and good-hearted.

Scott Roberts, after hearing the news, took it upon himself to search the hospital where he and Scott worked for anything that police might have missed. He focused on the IT department's data center and more specifically, he focused on the tile floor. He was able to lift up a tile using a suction cup, and underneath, found the item that would be pinned as the murder weapon: a hunting knife. He also discovered a pile of bloody clothes.

In November, 4 months after Thad's murder, Michelle and Scott were summoned to the court room for a preliminary hearing to decide who would be tried first.

"The state gets to elect, by law, who to try first. We had elected to try her first" said Patterson. The decision to try Michelle first was a risk, as her case was the weaker of the two. Prosecutors knew that she hadn't bene the one to physically take Thad's life, however, they held her responsible for the murder.

"She was the person that made it happen" said Ross Cavitt "even though Scott Harper had the murder weapon in his hand, they could see that he was following orders from Michelle which made her ultimately responsible for the crime."

The emails, although suspicious, didn't pin Michelle to giving the orders, but prosecutors hoped that Harper would. They hoped that by presenting him with the evidence that was quickly stacking against him, they would be able to convince him to cut a deal and turn his back on Michelle.

Aside from the leverage of evidence that prosecutors had, the DA had written and notified the court that she would be seeking the death penalty for both Scott and Michelle.

"After the death of a fine young man, a father of four, to seek the death penalty wasn't that surprising" said Cavitt, in regard to the DA's email.

All that was left for prosecutors to do was wait and hope that Scott would cave.

"I had begged Scotty to do what was needed and to give up the information, and to tell the story of his involvement and Michelle's involvement" Paige told Dateline "and he would always tell me no, to just leave her out of this"

"He was smitten and head over heels in love with her" Cavitt said.

"I think that she couldn't have cared less about him. I think he was just the muscle behind the act" said Patterson, who was convinced that Michelle had simply used Harper's infatuation with her to get him to do her bidding.

Despite the prosecutor's hopes, Harper continued to clam up when it came to Michelle's involvement. It seemed that even the threat of the death penalty wasn't enough to get him to talk.

Years passed this way.

"Meetings with him resulted in nothing. He would not come forward" said Staats.

Finally, in the fall of 2008 and 4 years after both parties had been locked behind bars, Scott was ready to cooperate with prosecutors.

Scott's attorneys helped him decide on a deal and upon this conversation, it became to clear to everyone involved that Harper was still infatuated with Michelle as his concern for her took center stage. He would take a life sentence and plead guilty, as long as the death penalty was taken off of Michelle's case. He did, however, agree to testify at Michelle's trial.

"He effectively saved and betrayed her at the same time" said one of his attorneys.

In the court room on October 1st, 2008, Harper sat with prosecutors and told them his account of Thad's death.

"He told us that he still loved her and he was going to do anything in his power to minimize her involvement" said Patterson

"Michelle had basically said that Thad would not leave easily. He would fight for her and not give up on their marriage and that it would get ugly" said another of his attorneys "and he said that he could deal with ugly."

After this conversation, according to Scott, he had purchased the hunting knife and the next day, he had had lunch with Michelle. The two had parked and kissed in the back seat like a pair of teenagers, and it was during this time that Michelle had asked him if he had talked to her husband yet. When he told her that he hadn't, Michelle withdrew her affection and became cold and distant towards him.

Scott said that he had been afraid of losing her, so four days later he had woken up before dawn and driven to the Frito Lay distribution center with the intent to deal with Thad Reynolds.

As he entered the building, Thad had looked up and asked him what he was doing there. Scott Harper had replied with "I want what you got."

Harper's story was not enough to pin the murder on Michelle: it was only enough to charge her with adultery.

"All it would take was for one person on the jury to say that okay. Maybe Michelle really did think that Scott was just going to talk to her husband" Patterson said.

On January 13th, 2010, Michelle was brought back into court after 6 years of being in jail. The officials and attorneys present had been expecting for Harper to testify against Michelle, however, this did not happen. Michelle stood before the jury and plead guilty to voluntary manslaughter.

"Getting Scott Harper's statement was like pulling teeth and she didn't think we'd get it. That's the only reason that she plead guilty"

" She knew that she was responsible for the death, in some way, because of the affair and because of that she felt that she should plead guilty to something" said Scott's attorney.

At the hearing that day, Thad's mother asked Michelle why her son had had to die for this.

"There was no response" said Thad's mother, Kittie Walker, "her eyes were just cold. No remorse, no feelings, nothing."

"She knew that Thad would not have let her take the kids away" said Beverly Owens "and she knew that that was the only way to get him out of the picture"

In the end, she was sentenced to 20 years behind bars, with credit being given to the time she had already served in county jail. Until her release, Michelle is unable to see her children and will lose custody of them.

According to Scott Roberts, there were people who upon hearing her sentencing, didn't feel as if justice had been served.

"I would have liked to see Michelle get a lot more time for it. I would have liked to see her life in prison" said Kittie Walker.

Many people in Rome, Georgia agreed that although Scott had wielded the knife, Michelle was the villain behind the plot.

"We're in a religious town and I think that many people believed that Scotty had been manipulated by her and that she was the devil incarnate" said Jim Berry.

Despite the tension and hard feelings, Paige Harper was visibly shaken by the case.

"Scott and Michelle were the two most important people in my life other than my kids, so for this to happen...it really makes me wonder how well I know people" she said.

In the aftermath of the murder, Thad's mother got custody of the kids and Paige divorced her husband in 2005. Despite writing letters in the early days of their sentences, Michelle and Scott have stopped communicating.

Within recent years, Michelle has written to officials asking why she isn't allowed to see her children.

"We do it all the time with adults- no contact with whomever. That's not anything new. That's a standard law order in nearly every murder case I've had, even if they're in the same family" responded Patterson, who also stated that Michelle is well aware of this order as it was part of her plea deal back in January of 2010.

Judge J. Bryant Durham, who had found Michelle guilty in years prior, mentioned that once her children turn 18 they can visit her in prison. Currently, this means that Michelle's eldest daughter, 22-year old Alisan and her infant grandchild can visit her in prison whenever they wish.

"Like it or not, if she decides to go over there every day, I don't think that can be stopped" Durham told Patterson.

The intent of the order was to restrict visitation until Michelle was released, however, due to lack of specifics and bad wording, the age of visitation remains 18.

There's no question that a good man died for less than good reasons, but there are still questions in the minds of his family and friends. Why had it happened? Had death really been Michelle's only option? It's up for speculation and, unfortunately, no one will ever know for sure.

HUSBAND KILLER : THE TRUE STORY OF MICHELLE HALL

TORI BAKER

It's never easy being a member of a blended family. There's a certain understanding that comes along with a second or third marriage – especially one involving children – that there is going to be a fundamental need for combined effort, tolerance and compromise.

When Michelle Garner remarried for what would be the third and last time, family and friends believed she had finally found happiness after reconnecting with an old high-school flame.

John Brittson "Britt" Hall, an aircraft mechanic and home builder, had known his own fair share of heartache; he was recently divorced when he found his old high school girlfriend, Michelle, on an online dating web site.

Britt Hall and Michelle Garner first met in 1986 while attending high school in Newnan, GA. The two briefly dated before Michelle Hall graduated in 1987.

"They both were in the popular clique," forensic psychologist Robert Brion said. "Britt was a baseball player that all of the girls had a crush on. Michelle was popular herself, very outgoing with a lot of friends."

The parents of Britt and Michelle were friends as well but they didn't consider the dating relationship between Michelle and Britt to be a serious one. After graduation, Michelle would move away and she would marry a man named Rusty Hart. The couple would have two daughters until their divorce in 1996.

The single mom worked as a dental assistant to support her daughters. Times were tight until 1999 when she met and married Steve Davis.

"Steve Davis was a businessman," Brion said. "He was divorced himself with a daughter of his own. He met Michelle and quickly fell for her charms as she could come across as a very warm and caring person. He asked her to marry him after about a year of dating."

Michelle would become pregnant during the union and give birth to her third daughter, Alyssa.

Unfortunately, her second marriage met the same fate as her first and within a few years, the couple had filed for divorce, citing irreconcilable differences.

Britt did well for himself after high school, becoming an airline mechanic for Delta Airlines. He made good money with Delta until they laid him off. He then went into business with his father in home construction until ultimately returning back to Delta after they had a rehire.

His marriage started to fail, however. His first wife cited that Britt had "mental problems" and filed for divorce, stating that the marriage was "irretrievably broken."

"Britt's first wife would take him to court at least six to eight times a year after their divorce," Brion said. "He was depressed and the court visits weren't helping."

His divorce would coincide with Michelle's impending divorce with Steve Davis. Her divorce with Davis was a particularly nasty one and Britt could sympathize. They would reconnect over a dating website.

In the midst of her own divorce, Garner was happy to find love again with Britt Hall as they rekindled old flames. Shortly after reconnecting, Britt invited Michelle over for Sunday lunch with his family, and all seemed well for the couple.

"Michelle did mention to Britt's family that she was going through some difficult times with her divorce," Brion said. "She was cheerful throughout but hinted that the custody battles she was going through were quite serious."

Little did Britt Hall's family know that their excitement would soon be turned to devastation; a tragedy that would make national headlines and be detailed in various murder documentaries.

THE BRADY BUNCH

Ronald Hall, Britt's father was all to happy to have Michelle back in his son's life. At least at first.

"We visited and talked," Ronald said. "And she came in and was just as happy as she ever was," he said.

It wasn't long before Britt Hall's romance with Garner turned more serious, and the two tied the knot in September of 2006. The new marriage was an adjustment, to say the least. Britt had three children from his previous marriage and Michelle Hall had three of her own children as well. The blended family of eight was now living in Britt Hall's town home.

"You can imagine how tight the living quarters were," Brion said. "But Michelle's girls really took to their new stepfather. They became comfortable enough to call him 'Dad.'"

Britt wanted a bigger home and decided to build a large home with the help of his father. The men paid for contractors to pour concrete and establish the foundation, but father and son built the majority of the house by hand.

"People didn't know where the couple were getting the money to build the house," Brion said. "But Britt did most of the work himself after the foundation was laid. So he was able to save a lot of money when it came to sweat equity. That's a testimony to how badly he wanted the marriage between he and Michelle to work out."

When all was said and done, Britt and Michelle Hall were the proud owners of a beautiful 4100 square foot home on ten acres, the perfect place to spend the rest of their lives together. The brand new house boasted vaulted ceilings, granite counter tops, and a finished basement. The construction would prove to be a house of cards, however, as things were brewing underneath the surface.

Michelle didn't have much luck with her two previous marriages, and although individual accounts may vary, her two former husbands are both to have reported being abused by Michelle during the course of their marriage.

Michelle never had a firm grasp on her emotions and didn't handle anger well. These character flaws would not bode well for her life with

Britt. Dealing with both partners' ex-spousal issues including custody and visitation, Michelle and Britt found themselves tinkering on the edge of divorce after a few months into their marriage.

"The way Britt and Michelle handled their issues were different," said family friend Sue Mathis. "Michelle was quicker to speak her mind and a lot of times, Britt just wanted her to try to gain a little bit more self-control."

Dealing with his own ex-wife and their similar divorce problems, Britt Hall was also facing his own internal battles with depression. Although he wasn't often the instigator in their frequent arguments, he was known to fervently engage in the verbal conflicts. While this certainly wasn't conducive to a happy and fruitful marriage, Britt Hall made it clear to friends he would not give up on his family and the life he had built.

The next couple of years came with continued stress, intensified by financial worries after the Halls realized they had gotten too far deep in debt as a result of building their dream home. Notices of foreclosure, liens on the house, and over-extensions were haunting the couple and causing both spouses to hit a breaking point.

On July 30, 2008, it was another typical tense day in the Hall household. Friends say Britt Hall, already aggravated due to a landscaper failing to complete a job on time, went to the store to pick-up hot dogs for a family get-together.

"Hey hon," Britt said as he called his wife. "How many hot dogs do you think I should get-"

"Count how many damn people are here," Michelle snapped. "That's how much you should get."

This would be the snide comeback that would break the straw in Britt's back. He grew tired at her constant bickering and baiting. When he came home that evening, a fight would ensue.

Michelle's youngest daughter, Alyssa, was in the living room watching television as her mother vacuumed to prepare for the company soon arriving. When Britt Hall told Alyssa to turn the TV down, another argument between the couple ensued and Hall immediately told her daughter to go upstairs to her bedroom and not come out until she was called.

There are only two individuals who know the details of what followed on that evening, and only one of them lived to tell. When all was said and done, Britt would be dead and Michelle would be charged with murder.

The 911 call came in at 8:02 p.m. by a frantic Michelle who told dispatchers that her husband had tried to kill her and commit suicide.

"He shot at me, and we were fighting to get it," Michelle told dispatchers regarding the weapon. She said she heard the gun go off twice. Seconds later, she told dispatchers her husband was turning blue.

When police arrived, Britt Hall was dead and had three noticeable gunshot wounds to his body: one on his left arm, one on his right thigh, and a close-range shot to his chest. Michelle Hall, bruised, scraped and covered in blood, told first responders the same story she had told dispatchers: her suicidal husband had tried to kill her before turning the gun on himself.

Prior to further investigation, deputies on the scene immediately called Britt Hall's parents and told them their son had committed suicide. The Halls refused to believe the news.

"Things just seemed to be going too good at this time in his life for him to have done that," said his mother, Charlene Hall. "I knew he didn't kill himself; I knew for a fact that didn't happen."

It didn't take long for police to begin seeing the crime scene a little differently than Michelle had described. Blood splatter and numerous bullet holes covered the downstairs bedroom, and a trail of blood led into the bathroom where Britt Hall's lifeless body now lay. If this was a suicide, there sure was a struggle beforehand.

Investigators gave Michelle the opportunity to explain the scene. She told how an argument between the couple turned violent when

Britt Hall threw her onto the bed. He immediately went into the study and she followed him.

Then she noticed the gun on the computer desk.

Knowing her husband was battling depression, she said she immediately became concerned with his safety, worried that he may use the gun to harm himself.

Michelle stated that she instinctively dove for the gun, and that's when Britt Hall reached for it as well and the two began struggling for possession.

After both Michelle and her husband lost control of he gun, she quickly picked up the weapon and began shooting rounds into the walls and floor in an effort to unload the gun.

In the hall, Britt Hall caught up with her and that's when she said he threatened to kill her. In yet another entanglement of an attempt for control of the gun, Michelle said the gun accidentally went off. This shot punctured Britt Hall's thigh, and that's when Hall claimed she went to call for help.

Britt Hall began crawling into the bathroom, unable to walk and calling out her name for help. When she approached him, gun in hand, she said he grabbed the pistol from her, put it to his chest, and pulled the trigger.

The problem with her story, however, was that most suicides don't entail multiple gunshot wounds. Additionally, the manner in which the fatal shot was delivered raised eyebrows for investigators.

"I've worked many suicides in my career, and I've never worked a suicide that I can remember where a man had shot himself in the chest," Lt John Lewis said.

Furthermore, the gunshot wound on Britt Hall's chest had no signs of charring or burning around the entry wound, signs which usually indicate a self-inflicted wound.

Britt Hall also had a shattered elbow and a bullet hole in his left arm. Three different shots, all which led investigators to believe they weren't being told the whole story.

Michelle did her best to persuade the investigative team to believe her story, but her story changed upon being brought to the station for questioning. While at first she claimed the two struggled for control over the gun, she then claimed Britt Hall was never actually in possession of the gun at all.

Coupled with the evidence at the crime scene and her story's inconsistencies, Michelle was charged the next morning with the murder of her husband.

Crucial to the prosecution's case was the testimony of Michelle's youngest daughter, Alyssa, who was in the home during the shooting. Police brought the 8-year-old in for questioning immediately following the incident and she clearly stated she heard her step-father pleading with her mother to "put the gun down," she said. Alyssa would ultimately testify in her mother's trial in 2009.

Facing charges of malice murder and aggravated assault, Michelle vehemently denied killing her husband. She insisted that he died of a self-inflicted gunshot wound after threatening suicide and fighting with her over the .38 caliber revolver.

The fight that evening was par for the course, she said. The two regularly got into verbal and physical altercations, and their marriage was falling apart due to financial stress. They would also constantly fight over ex-spouses, custody and visitation regarding the six children. Although there were no police reports relating to any domestic altercations in the home before, family and friends knew things weren't okay on the home front.

"Britt would spend several nights driving to work calling me and saying 'I don't know what to do.' He would have done everything in his power to save his marriage, even if it was not worth saving. He was terrified of failure," said Mathis.

One of the first fights that turned physical in front of the family was in November 2006, when Britt Hall's eldest daughter came into the room to find Michelle Hall unconscious. Her father quickly ushered her out of the room and told her not to worry about it. The next couple of years only brought more trouble due to the same old problems and Britt's alleged mental illness.

Britt was prescribed three different types of medication for depression at the time of his death, police confirmed.

But the physical evidence did not add up to suicide. Initially, the Georgia Bureau of Investigation estimated the fatal gunshot to have been fired from around 18-24 inches away. This is not consistent with suicide, detectives argued. While many victims of mental illness fall prey to suicide each year, the facts must add up. In this case, they did not.

If convicted, Michelle was facing life in prison.

In September of 2009, testimonies were heard by Alyssa Davis, as well as responding officers Capt. Tony Grant and Sgt. Freddy Cox, about what they saw and heard on the night of the shooting.

Cox testified that Hall's appearance was "consistent with someone who'd been in a physical altercation" and that Hall had bruises, scrapes and blood on her neck and forehead as well as blood on her hands and a knot on her elbow.

During his testimony, Grant stated he immediately noticed that Hall's face was red and she had what appeared to be gun-shot residue on her hand, even though she was stating her husband had committed suicide.

There were multiple bullet holes throughout the downstairs of the home when police arrived on the scene, Grant testified. Two bullets were recovered from Britt Hall's body and three more were found in the house.

Grant said a blood pattern analysis showed blood spatters of 90 degrees in the downstairs quarters outside of the bathroom, proof that Britt Hall crawled into the bathroom after being wounded.

Defense Attorney Mike Kam said that while in no uncertain terms would he call the key ear witness a liar, her age and her location during the shooting did not make for the most reliable testimony.

"She was eight; she didn't see anything, she clearly got some of the facts confused." Kam said in an interview. "She's not someone who is used to being asked questions in formal interview settings. Who knows what she remembered, or what happened?"

Additionally, Kam indicated that Michelle certainly didn't fit the description of a murderer. Outside of two divorces, Hall had no criminal record. She was law-abiding citizen, with nothing in her background which would give the assumption she was capable of murder, he said.

But the jury had heard enough. On September 25, 2009, Michelle Hall was found guilty on all counts in the death of her husband Britt.

Not long after her conviction, Hall's attorneys filed a motion for a new trial, citing trial court errors. Coweta County Superior Court Judge Jack Kirby denied the motion and the defense attorneys took the case to the Supreme Court.

On September 22, 2010, the Supreme Court of Georgia upheld the conviction, despite Hall's defense's argument that the trial court erred by admitting similar transaction evidence and prior consistent statements.

Hall's defense stated that testimony from both of her ex-husbands that she was verbally and physically abusive were inadmissible because they were not "sufficiently similar" to establish proof of the crimes for which she was charged, according to the opinion of the Supreme Court. It also stated that "in cases of domestic violence, prior incidents of abuse against family members or sexual partners are more generally permitted because there is a logical connection between violent acts against two different persons with whom the accused had a similar emotional or intimate attachment."

The opinion also added that the fifteen and thirteen-year lapses of time between her ex-husband's allegations of abuse to the alleged shooting of her husband did not require exclusion of evidence.

"Given that the similar transaction evidence reflects appellant's behavior towards prior spouses, we conclude that any prejudice from the age of these prior incidents was outweighed by the probative value of the evidence under the particular facts of this case and the purpose for which the similar transactions were offered."

Eighteen months later, however, Michelle retained a new attorney who filed a habeas corpus petition, stating Michelle was given ineffective legal counsel by Kam during her trial in 2009. Senior Judge Robert B. Struble presided over the hearing and determined that Hall was in-fact entitled to a new trial. Struble agreed that Kam, Hall's trial attorney, was "ineffective and fell below the minimum guarantee of representation under the constitution," a press release said.

While Michelle may have been looking forward to another chance at redemption, The Attorney General's Office quickly announced their plans to appeal the habeas corpus ruling to the Georgia Supreme Court.

In a press release on March 30, 2012, Coweta County District Attorney Peter John Skandalakis expressed his respectful disapproval of the court's ruling and that in stating Kam was ineffective for representation, "the court erroneously applied the wrong standard under the law."

Skandalakis said he was optimistic that the Supreme Court will conclude that Hall had a legally sufficient defense and that her conviction would be upheld after review of the appeal.

On January 22, 2013, the Supreme Court found Hall's convictions to be fair and just, denying insufficient representation during her 2009 trial. According to the court summary, the Supreme Court concluded that the habeas corpus petition did not conduct proper legal analysis to determine the effectiveness of Hall's defense.

The opinion references Strickland v. Washington, a 1984 Supreme Court case in which it determined that to be granted a new trial, a defendant must show that it was due to insufficient performance by defense that the defendant was found guilty.

Michelle's argument for her habeas corpus petition was that "if she were in the same room when her young daughter was questioned, she could have assisted her attorney by prompting him with specific information," the court says in its opinion. However, it was determined during the habeas hearing that any information she would have portrayed to her attorney was already known information to both parties. "As such, Hall has failed to show actual prejudice, and her claim of ineffective assistance of counsel should have been rejected," the opinion said.

Today, Michelle Hall remains in a Coweta County prison.

Since her conviction, Michelle's ex-husbands have been given full custody of her three respective daughters.

She won't be eligible for parole until 2039. She will be 70 years old.

Milton Keynes UK
Ingram Content Group UK Ltd.
UKHW040639131024
449481UK00001B/51